About Island Press

Island Press is the only nonprofit organization in the
United States whose principal purpose is the publication
of books on environmental issues and natural resource
management. We provide solutions-oriented information
to professionals, public officials, business and community
leaders, and concerned citizens who are shaping responses
to environmental problems.

In 2004, Island Press celebrates its twentieth anniver-
sary as the leading provider of timely and practical books
that take a multidisciplinary approach to critical environmental concerns. Our growing list of titles reflects our
commitment to bringing the best of an expanding body
of literature to the environmental community throughout
North America and the world.

Support for Island Press is provided by the Agua Fund,
Brainerd Foundation, Geraldine R. Dodge Foundation,
Doris Duke Charitable Foundation, Educational
Foundation of America, The Ford Foundation, The
George Gund Foundation, The William and Flora
Hewlett Foundation, Henry Luce Foundation, The John
D. and Catherine T. MacArthur Foundation, The Andrew
W. Mellon Foundation, The Curtis and Edith Munson
Foundation, National Environmental Trust, The New-
Land Foundation, Oak Foundation, The Overbrook
Foundation, The David and Lucile Packard Foundation,
The Pew Charitable Trusts, The Rockefeller Foundation,
The Winslow Foundation, and other generous donors.

The opinions expressed in this book are those of the
authors and do not necessarily reflect the views of these
foundations.

The New Consumers

The New Consumers

The Influence of Affluence on the Environment

Norman Myers and Jennifer Kent

ISLAND PRESS

Washington • Covelo • London

Library of Congress Cataloging-in-Publication data.
Myers, Norman.
The New Consumers : the influence of affluence
on the environment / Norman Myers and Jennifer Kent.
p. cm.
Includes bibliographical references and index.
ISBN 1-55963-997-0 (cloth : alk. paper)
1. Economic development—Environmental aspects.
2. Consumption (Economics)—Environmental aspects.
3. Sustainable development. 4. Environmental responsibility.
I. Kent, Jennifer. II. Title.
HD75.6.M48 2004
333.71'3—dc22
2004004202

British Cataloguing-in-Publication data available.

Printed on recycled, acid-free paper

Design by David Bullen

Manufactured in the United States of America

10 9 8 7 6 5 4 3 2 1

To those many colleagues who inspired the authors along their way, and to all those who would like to keep on consuming indefinitely rather than over-consuming for a short while.

Contents

List of Tables and Figures

Preface

THIS HAS BEEN quite the most complex and taxing of all my eighteen books. Or rather, all our recent books because the cover features the name of my co-author and partner Jennifer Kent. Without her, there would simply have been no book. Jennie has dug out most of the statistics, she has analyzed them into shape, she has Googled all manner of other information and insights, she has read and re-re-read chapter drafts, and she has kept a firm hold on the entire exercise when it wanted to turn into a dozen jellyfishes. All I had to do was to write the book, which was quite straightforward as compared with my co-author's role. And she has proffered mountains of patience while dealing with my impatience. Ah, what it is to live in a world with miracles.

I shall shortly complete my seventieth circuit of the sun, and I have spent nigh on thirty of my years in developing countries. I have watched them develop until certain sectors of certain countries have become distinctly middle class. Sizeable numbers of their citizens have left behind the abject poverty that still afflicts most of their compatriots, and these "new consumers" are transforming the economic and social landscapes of their countries. They are also transforming the political landscape of the global order. If, for instance, China keeps up its twenty-year-long achievement of record-breaking economic growth, we shall soon—within less than twenty years—see it as the biggest economy as well as the biggest populace in the world. By that time too, China and just another four new consumer countries could account for fully one-fifth of the global economy as measured in terms of "purchasing power parity." Truly, the world it is a-changin'. It will be a-changin' too in environmental senses. The new consumers can eat meat every day at least, instead of once a week at most, and feedlot production methods are placing heavy pressures on supplies of grain and water. The new consumers are also buying cars in large numbers, with all that means for pollution both local and global. For sure, the new consumers should enjoy their new found affluence to the hilt, provided that does not mean unsustainable demands on environments, hence on economies too, of many a sort. In turn this means there is all the greater urgency in establishing what is known as sustainable consumption, especially on the part of the long-rich consumers in developed countries—who could thereby pave the way for the new consumers.

I have thought that it would be worthwhile to describe this new consumer phenomenon in a book. At first I found few people interested. Manila, is that simply a kind of envelope? Jeddah, is that a new sort of dessert? But then I came across Jonathan Cobb at Island Press, and he instantly took me on. Throughout a protracted and convoluted process, he has helped me untangle one problem after another after another. Many thanks, Jonathan.

Earlier on, the basic idea was welcomed too by Wren Wirth of the Winslow Foundation, who encouraged me to research the issue and write up my findings in a report that her foundation funded. Without you, Wren, the whole thing would not even have got onto the start line. I am specially grateful for your once-again support.

I also appreciate the efforts of my literary agent, Ginger Barber. This is the umpetty-eth book she has handled for me, and she has done it in her invariably proficient fashion. I have long been fortunate to have such a fine colleague to bear my banner into the publishing lists.

Finally, here's a thought from my co-author Jennie. "This is to be my final book (I said that three books ago). It has been a long and arduous task, with mountains of background research, analysis, editing, and endless re-editing. I hope the result fosters better all-round futures for those who will be around to experience them, among the most important for me being my sons Mathew and Andrew. I hope too they will finally understand what my efforts have been all about. It has taken me several decades to learn the true value of my life, and ever-more consumption—it isn't even a starter."

Norman Myers and Jennifer Kent
December 2003

The New Consumers

Who Are the New Consumers?

WE ARE WITNESSING one of the biggest revolutions in history. Something hugely important is afoot in the world, yet many people seem little aware of it. It makes few headlines on television or in newspapers. It does not advertise its arrival, even though it will markedly affect all our lives in both economic and environmental senses.

It is the biggest consumer boom ever known in such a short time. It is not occurring, as might be supposed, in the long-rich countries, but in certain developing and transition countries where over 1 billion people now possess the financial muscle to enjoy a consumerist lifestyle. This is not to overlook that there are also 2.8 billion people in the world who subsist on less than $2 a day, 1.2 billion of them on less than $1 a day. Poverty remains the lot of almost half of humankind. But now, and for the first time, there is a sizeable community of people outside the long-rich countries who have clambered up the ladder into the middle classes and are enjoying a measure of affluence.

Consumption: it's what we want, all of us. We follow a deep-seated tradition that began 10,000 years ago when people moved on from a hunter-gatherer existence and settled in villages where they began to find ways to expand their lifestyles. It has been a realistic tradition. Until a century or two back, virtually all people have been preoccupied from dawn till dusk and from birth till death in keeping body and soul together. Since they have found it hard to meet even the most

basic needs, their credo has been that more of anything must, by def-
inition, be a good thing. Result: a seeking after ever-greater consumption, indeed limitless consumption. To cite the economics guru Adam
Smith, "Consumption is the sole end and purpose of all production."[1]

Today's new consumers no doubt feel they are participating in that
same age-old tradition, especially since it reflects the holy grail to
which all the new consumers aspire, a Western lifestyle. Also without
doubt is that they are consuming as fast and as variously as they can,
although most still have a very long way to go before catching up with
North American and Western European lifestyles. All the new consumers have reached a level of affluence where they can satisfy not
only every basic need but some luxuries as well. Many of them have
reached a still higher level of affluence where they can indulge in a
lifestyle of outright prosperity. All such consumers enjoy decent diets.
They have moved beyond functional clothing to fashionable attire.
They purchase throw-away products rather than unpackaged goods.
Many of them eschew public transport in favor of the car. The wealthier ones live in air-conditioned and single-family homes rather than
in modest and naturally ventilated homes, and in the company of
extended or multiple families.[2] And of course they are wholly entitled
to follow their proclivities, provided their consumption does not levy
environmental costs that could undercut their prospects for still
greater consumption, or the prospects of those fellow citizens who
are still trying to set foot on the affluence ladder.

All too often, however, today's headlong consumption—whether
in new consumer countries or, more pertinently, in the long-rich
countries—means environmental problems such as grandscale pollution, waste mountains, energy shortages, land degradation, water
deficits, even climate upheavals.[3] All of us contribute to these problems. A visit to the shopping mall often means more "stuff" with
excess piled on excess in the hunt for a life that is better off though not
always better. All of us want to put our car on the road, thus adding to
traffic congestion and pollution. Even saints produce their share of
rubbish. Of course such environmental troubles have arisen chiefly in

the so-called developed countries, the ones that have enjoyed fattest-cat lifestyles for decades. The new consumers are doing no more than follow a well-beaten path.

Recall how far our present consumption patterns are unsustainable, and by a long and lengthening way. We already consume over half of all available freshwater. By 2020 we shall have another 1.3 billion people on top of today's 6.3 billion, all looking for their "fair share" of limited water supplies—and many of them will likely be making still greater demands on every last precious drop. So tough is this prospect that certain policy leaders—not eco-alarmists—anticipate there could be water wars ahead.[4] We are also consuming or otherwise co-opting so much of Earth's net plant growth that we leave less than half for the millions of other species. We have degraded 20 million square kilometers of land, an expanse equivalent to more than twice the United States. We are even dislocating our climate systems.

There are many other signs that our consumption is depleting the environmental resource base that underpins all our economies, our societies, our futures. A recent overview analysis shows that in 1960 we were exploiting 70% of our planet's resources, a figure that by 1999 had risen to 120%.[5] We are bumping our heads against the ceiling with ever-greater vigor. The Rio Earth Summit in 1992 issued a wake-up call to alert us to the imperative of environmental safeguards, yet by the time of the World Summit on Sustainable Development in 2002 the number of people lacking safe drinking water had risen from 1.1 billion to 1.2 billion, tropical forests were being destroyed faster than ever, deserts were expanding faster than ever, and carbon dioxide (CO_2) emissions had increased by 12%. Plus, the number of people enduring absolute poverty had risen from 1.1 billion to 1.3 billion. True, the annual increase in human numbers had declined from 90 million to around 80 million, but that still leaves a long way to go before we achieve zero population growth.

Of course there is nothing intrinsically wrong with affluent communities consuming a large share of natural resources if those resources remain plentiful and can be recycled. For iron and steel, 85% is

consumed by the top 20% of people worldwide, 55% being recycled—
and the top 20% do not thereby crucially limit the consumption of
poor people. Indeed, the affluent communities' conversion of natural
resources into human capital often enhances human welfare all round.
It would be of scant consequence that the average American consumes 80 times as much paper as the average Indian, were the American to recycle most of the paper (at present, only 45%). Much more
significant is that the average American consumes 240 times as
much gasoline as the average Indian, and thus contributes far more to
CO_2 emissions and global warming processes.[6] The key question is
whether consumption uses resources or uses them up.

Overall, then, there is a strong environmental significance to the
arrival of the new consumers. To repeat: they are as entitled as anyone
to enjoy their newfound affluence. That is a given from the start, and
a given to be surrounded with neon flashing lights. At the same time,
the new consumers should restrain the environmental injury they
inflict on their own countries and those farther afield. Just their cars,
one-fifth of the global fleet in 2000 and likely to total almost one-third
as soon as 2010, make a sizeable contribution to the atmospheric
buildup of CO_2, which accounts for half of global warming. Thus the
new consumers have an impact not only on their own societies but on
the worldwide community. For sure, the biggest car contribution to
global warming still lies with the long-rich countries, and during the
1990s the 43 million additional rich-world people polluted the planet
more than the 760 million additional people in developing countries.
But the new consumers could heed the many other downside lessons
of the car culture in Los Angeles, London, Rome, and other congested
cities of the so-called developed countries.

There are further economic costs of consumerism's spread, even
though the new consumers are major drivers of their countries' economies. Water shortages limit agriculture and industry. Pollution levies
its tolls through health problems. There are many other examples, all
too familiar. In Thailand's capital, Bangkok, traffic gridlock with drivers' lost time and wasted gasoline costs the city's economy $4 billion

per year (though only one-quarter as much as in Los Angeles). There are large costs from road congestion and traffic pollution in many other new-consumer cities such as Seoul, Hong Kong, Jakarta and Sao Paulo.[7] As the reader will find in this book, the economic downside of runaway consumption is sizeable already, and it is growing bigger fast.

In short, the phenomenon of the new consumers should alert us all to what could well prove to be the biggest challenge ahead: how to achieve ever-greater consumption—or, better consumption of alternative sorts—without grossly depleting the environmental underpinnings of our economies? Fortunately, and as this book demonstrates with examples aplenty, there are a lot of ways we can measure up to the challenge—and we shall surely find it will lead to lifestyles more streamlined and fulfilling than anything we have known to date (plus, a more discerning approach will often put money into our pockets). If we can all—each and every one of us—contain and eventually reduce the adverse impacts of consumption, that could well rank as the finest environmental success story to date.

Definition of the New Consumers

Before we consider the degree of affluence that defines the new consumers, we shall look at a couple of economic factors that are crucial to the entire reckoning. First is the historical yardstick of Gross National Product (GNP), reflecting the economic value of all goods and services produced in a country, and thus serving as a very rough indicator of how all the country's citizens are faring. In recent years the GNP label has been widely replaced as an economic measure by Gross National Income (GNI).

Secondly, GNP and GNI have traditionally been expressed in conventional or international-exchange dollars, which have failed to reveal true purchasing power. An alternative and more realistic measurement is "purchasing power parity" (PPP) dollars,[8] which in 20 select countries (see table I.1) are between 1.4 and 5.2 times greater than conventional dollars. In India, for example, per-capita GNI in

2002 was a low $480, but in PPP terms it was $2570, a reflection of the lower cost of goods and services in India relative to the United States. In other words, $480 in India would buy purchases worth almost $2600 in the United States. At a New York supermarket a banana may well cost 25 cents, but on a New Delhi street the same sum would purchase half a dozen bananas. A New York taxi ride for $5 would take you only a fraction as far as its New Delhi counterpart.

Thus the PPP adjustment provides an indicator of people's well-being that is comparable across countries, free of the exchange rate and price distortions that arise when GNI is converted through conventional international-exchange rates. In China the 2002 figures were $940 and PPP$4390, in Brazil $2850 and PPP$7250, and in Russia $2140 and PPP$7820. Conversely, in many countries of Western Europe, also Japan, with their higher costs of living relative to the United States, GNI/PPP can be lower than GNI converted at conventional-dollar rates. In Switzerland the figures were $37,930 and PPP$31,250, and in Japan $33,550 and PPP$26,070. A conventional-dollar assessment shows that in 2002 an average Japanese was 36 times richer than an average Chinese, but PPP-based figures show that he or she was less than 6 times richer.[9] Whether in conventional dollars or PPP dollars, the United States remains the world's biggest economy, but the PPP reckoning means that China jumps from sixth to second and India from eleventh to fourth. Whereas Indonesia and Turkey do not make the top 20 economies in conventional dollars, in PPP dollars they are fifteenth and nineteenth (see table I.1).

Now to define the new consumers. They are people within an average of four-member households who possess purchasing power of at least PPP$10,000 per year, or at least PPP$2500 per person. These cut-off figures may seem a trifle arbitrary, but they are no more so than a parallel categorization in developed countries. These countries' governments have long divided their citizens into socioeconomic classes known as A, B, C through to F classes that roughly correspond to rich, upper-middle, middle, lower-middle, low and lowest classes. While such classifications may seem to some eyes as if they have been plucked out of the air, there is much sound analysis behind them, and in any case they are necessary for all manner of national planning purposes.

There are other considerations in support of the figures defining new consumers. While they are a tad too technical to be dealt with here, they are available to the interested reader in appendix A.

The PPP$10,000 household level is a minimum estimate, and most new consumers possess purchasing power way higher, often several times more. The basic figures are used here because they mark the rough stage when people start to engage in a distinctly middle-class lifestyle. As people climb the income ladder, they buy televisions, refrigerators, washing machines, air conditioners, and electronics such as hi-fi equipment and personal computers, among other perquisites

TABLE I.I: **The World's 20 Largest Economies in 2002**

	$, billions		PPP$, billions
USA	10,138	USA	10,138
Japan	3979	China	5732
Germany	1976	Japan	3261
UK	1552	India	2695
France	1410	Germany	2172
China	1237	France	1554
Italy	1181	UK	1511
Canada	716	Italy	1481
Spain	650	Brazil	1312
Mexico	637	Russia	1142
India	515	Canada	902
South Korea	477	Mexico	879
Brazil	452	Spain	852
Netherlands	414	South Korea	784
Australia	411	Indonesia	664
Russia	347	Australia	544
Switzerland	268	South Africa	442
Belgium	248	Netherlands	440
Sweden	230	Turkey	430
Austria	203	Thailand	418
Totals	*27,041		**37,353
World	32,253		47,426

Source: World Bank, World Development Indicators 2003 Database
(http://www.worldbank.org/data/wdi2003/index.htm)

*These 20 countries, with 6 new-consumer countries, account for 84% of the global economy.
**These 20 countries, with 10 new-consumer countries, account for 79% of the global PPP economy.

of an affluent lifestyle. They shift to a diet strongly based on meat, especially grain-fed meat. They consume large amounts of water, not only in their homes but via grainland irrigation. As they clamber still farther up the income ladder, they buy cars, often the fancier models.[10] Many of these purchases carry only moderate environmental impacts, but it is electricity-driven household appliances, meat, and cars and that spell the biggest environmental trouble.

Note the particular impact of cars. As mentioned, the 1.1 billion new consumers in 2000 possessed one-fifth of the global fleet, or 125 million cars. The recent growth rate has been so high that by 2010 they could have 250 million cars, or almost one-third of the global fleet. Between 1990 and 1997, CO_2 emissions from the world's motor vehicles, of which cars made up three-quarters, increased by one-quarter, four times faster than CO_2 emissions from all sources. Cars are expected to make up the fastest growing sector of energy use as far ahead as 2025.[11] They also cause much local pollution and severe road congestion among other problems.

For sure, the pattern of consumption varies from country to country, just as the amount of consumption varies according to the amount of income and spending power. But the picture above serves to reflect the situation in new-consumer countries as a whole. On the basis of the first author's travel and work in dozens of countries around the world during the past four decades, the picture can be taken to be simplified without being simplistic. A more accurate cut-off level could turn out to be rather more, whether for households or individuals. But the estimates of PPP$10,000 and PPP$2500 are supported by much on-the-ground evidence, and they seem acceptable for present purposes. Moreover—and to reiterate a crucial point—the cut-off levels cited are minimum levels, and most new consumers receive incomes a good deal higher, some enjoying incomes several times higher.

This latter factor reflects what is technically known as skewedness of income. More citizens make it into affluence than a simple reckoning of per-capita GNI would suggest—just as many citizens enjoy less than the per-capita average. In 16 of the 20 new-consumer countries, the top one-fifth of the population enjoys half or more of national income, and in all of them two-fifths of the population enjoy three-fifths or more. Plainly these are the shares of population that contain most new consumers. In Brazil in the late 1990s, the top 40% enjoyed 82% of GNI, the bottom 40% just 8%. In South Africa, the figures were 83% and 8%, and in Russia 74% and 13% (in the United States, 69% and 16%). At the other end of the scale, South Korea, Pakistan, Indonesia, and Poland's top 40% enjoyed 62% of GNI, and Ukraine's 61%[12] (see figure I.1).

In 10 countries, moreover, the "top of the pile" people generally showed growing concentration of affluence and hence of consumption during the 1990s ("To him that hath shall be given"). In Poland the top 20% enjoyed 37% of GNI in 1992, rising to 40% in 1998; in India 41% in 1990 and 46% in 1997; and in China 42% in 1990 and 47% in 1998. Conversely there was a decline in several countries that suffered financial setbacks, albeit transient ones, notably South Korea, Thailand, Brazil, Venezuela, and Russia.[13]

Finally, the reader is asked to bear in mind that a book stuffed with statistics will feature variations in accuracy and precision. No agencies such as the World Bank or the United Nations publish statistics for the new consumers, indicating whether they are moderately or highly affluent and whether they make up a majority or a minority of various countries' populations. True, there is documentation of how many people are in the top income categories in particular countries, but that does not tell us about how much they earn and whether they qualify for new-consumer status as defined above. It is curious that the leading international agencies have not done more to assess the major phenomenon represented by the new consumers, but that is a story for another day.

Fortunately the agencies offer stacks of statistics on GNI, household consumption, PPP equivalents, economic growth rates, country populations, and income distributions. The authors have mined these rich ores of statistics to calculate percentiles of populations at various

FIGURE I.I. **Income Distribution, late 1990s**

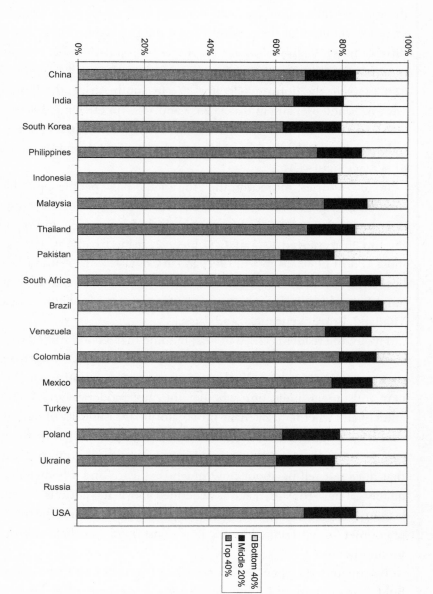

income levels, in order to come up with estimates of new-consumer numbers in the years 2000 and 2010.[14] In the main, these estimates are considered correct within 5% either way, and many of them better than that. Only a very few should be viewed as 10% uncertain. There is further uncertainty at work in that such a new field features information gaps and there is far from total documentation. But the authors believe they have pinned down enough chunks of crucial information that they are justified in sometimes proceeding by "joining up the dots."

Emergence of the New Consumers

How long have the new consumers been around and where do they now live? In 1980 there was still an obvious divide between the developed world and the developing world, these being polite labels for the rich world and the poor world. The rich people (North America, Western Europe, Japan, and Australasia) had an average per-capita GNI of $10,700, which meant they enjoyed affluent lifestyles. The poor people, by contrast, had per-capita GNIs averaging $370, which meant that most of them were merely enduring their lifestyles. There was a rich/poor gulf so large that it was difficult to comprehend—and today it is twice as much again even after allowing for a PPP adjustment. Moreover, a figure of $10,700 in 1980 may seem meagre to a year 2004 reader. Bear in mind, however, that prices and values change a lot in a quarter century. An equivalent sum in 2002 would have been $23,400.[15] To put things in further proportion, note that the official U.S. poverty line for a four-person family in 2002 was $18,100.

From the early 1980s onwards there was a start on a new trend. There began to emerge sizeable numbers of people in the developing world who were making it big style, at least in comparison with what they had known before. They were prominent in South Korea, Malaysia, Thailand, Iran, Saudi Arabia, Brazil, Venezuela, and Mexico. By the late 1980s these new consumers probably totaled a few hundred million. This was not many compared with the 850 million consumers in the rich countries, but it was a big jump over what had gone before.

For decades and in fact centuries, the developing countries had been virtually wall-to-wall "have-nots," with only a scattering of fortunates who could qualify as "haves." By the late 1980s many of these countries featured the first flickerings of haves in notable numbers. That still did not offer portent, however, of the explosive outburst of people mounting the affluence ladder during the 1990s.

A similar experience overtook the transition countries of Eastern Europe and the former Soviet Union. They are termed "transition" because, following the collapse of the Soviet empire in 1991, they started to switch from socialist to capitalist economies. They began to feature a strongly growing middle class, albeit not until a decade after the breakthrough in certain developing countries.

This outburst of new-consumer affluence became apparent in the form of modern housing, designer goods, fashion clothing, quality restaurants, department stores, international hotels, classy cars and other perquisites of Western lifestyles. On his travels this book's first author could see in Bangkok executive-style houses, semiluxury shops, and high-cost electronics on many a side, plus other conspicuous markers of "We've made it." Not all today's new consumers enjoy such fancy lifestyles, indeed the majority are more moderate consumers, but all are worlds beyond the impoverished lot of their fellow citizens. In Beijing he could well credit the story that this was becoming the number-one market for Mercedes cars outside Germany, and in Rio de Janeiro that its neon-lit streets and glitzy skylines bespoke large numbers of people who were doing all right, thanks very much. In Kuala Lumpur he noted the luxurious Shuria shopping center, and in India he heard that shopping malls have increased from 20 in 1999 to 150 today. In Moscow he has seen many people sporting Hermes scarves, Prada handbags, and Rolex watches. In Shanghai he has noted branches of such household-goods giants as America's Home Depot, Sweden's Ikea, Germany's Obi, and Britain's B & Q. He came across similar indications in Seoul, Riyadh, Bogota, Mexico City, and Istanbul. The new consumers were sampling the high life, and they wanted to be seen to be doing so.[16]

By 2000 there were 1.1 billion of these people, with 945 million in 17 developing countries and 115 million in three transition countries. They totaled way more than the 850 million of the rich world, though with affluence generally far behind. They amounted to almost one-fifth of all citizens of the developing world, whereupon the label "developing world" became a distinct misnomer. Here was the biggest sunburst of affluence the world had ever seen in such a short period. It was far beyond what occurred at the start of the Middle Ages, the arrival of the Renaissance, or the emergence of the Industrial Revolution—or even the onset of rich-world prosperity in the 1950s.

Some examples: In 1970 South Korea's per-capita GNI (in current dollars—PPP$ had not yet been devised) was $260, in 1980 it was $1780, in 1990 it was $5740, and in 2002 it was $9930. Almost as much of a compressed rush to riches was Malaysia's, advancing from a per-capita GNI of $400 in 1970 to $1830 in 1980, to $2380 in 1990 and to $3540 in 2002. Equally startling has been China's experience, from $120 in 1970 and $220 in 1980 to $320 in 1990 and $940 in 2002. In 1980 China had few new consumers at all and in 1990 only a few tens of millions, but after almost a tripling of the economy during the 1990s—yes, true!—there were at least 300 million new consumers in 2000. Note that these financial totals were all in conventional dollars, whereas the alternative PPP reckoning would have doubled them or even tripled them, occasionally hiking them still higher. Note too that these totals applied to all citizens countrywide, whereas the new consumers would have been much more affluent than the national average.

At least as remarkable is that the new consumers' numbers today are generally growing faster than ever, so that their total may soar by half within the current decade. Still more startling again is that the collective spending power of today's new consumers already approaches that of the United States in PPP terms.

Not all the new consumers are truly new. While the great bulk have arrived in just the last two decades, a minority are old stagers. Argentina in the 1930s was wealthier than Greece, until it slipped off the development train and subsided into semipenury with only a relative handful of middle classers, let alone upper classers. Parts of southern Brazil today are as industrialized and affluent as Portugal, and have long harbored fair numbers of well-to-do people, whereas much of northern Brazil remains impoverished. Many urban Russians were doing okay-ish even before the demise of the Soviet Union, and despite the temporary economic collapse of the late 1990s they are now enjoying a fair degree of affluence. In any case, a sizeable sector of the Russian economy is made up of black market and other criminal activities, none of which are recorded in the official economy, so Russia with its "gangster capitalism" may be a poor country with a lot of rich people. South Africa, the sole new-consumer country in Africa, has long had a prosperous community of whites and semiprosperous communities of Asians and so-called Coloureds, who are now being joined by fast-growing numbers of making-it blacks.

Who, specifically who, are the new consumers? Long-standing members of the middle and upper classes can include senior managers, small business owners, investment bankers, physicians, lawyers, marketing executives, real estate agents, Internet engineers, architects, journalists, private school teachers, home designers, and insurance salespeople. More recent members can include computer programmers, junior managers, accountants, bank tellers, secretaries, and many others of similar status.

To check on the basic criteria: a new-consumer country has had a record of fast economic growth, generally averaging 5% per year for 10 years (the United States averaged only 3.4% during the 1990s), together with a population of at least 20 million people. The 20 new-consumer countries are, in Asia, China, India, South Korea, Philippines, Indonesia, Malaysia, Thailand, Pakistan, Iran, and Saudi Arabia. In Africa there is just South Africa. In Latin America there are Brazil, Argentina, Venezuela, Colombia, and Mexico. In Eastern Europe there are Turkey, Poland, Ukraine, and Russia. All of these countries have had vigorous if not booming economies (except for, in some instances, the transient financial meltdowns of the late 1990s), and they have populations of at least 20 million people—two factors that together mean they have large numbers of new consumers. Most notable is China with nearly 1.3 billion people, plus a recent economic growth rate of more than 10% per year, and 300 million new consumers. Something the same applies to India with almost 1.1 billion people today, plus a recent economic growth rate of more than 6% per year and 130 million new consumers. These two countries alone account for two-fifths of all new consumers in the 20 countries (see table I.2).

TABLE I.2 **The New Consumers in 2000**

Country	Population, millions	Per-capita GNI, $s	Per-capita GNI, PPP$s	New consumers, millions (and % of population)	New consumers' purchasing power,* PPP$ billions (and % of national total)
China	1262	840	3920	303 (24)	1267 (52)
India	1016	450	2340	132 (13)	609 (39)
South Korea	47	8910	17300	45 (96)	502 (99)
Philippines	76	1040	4220	33 (43)	150 (75)
Indonesia	210	570	2830	63 (30)	288 (56)
Malaysia	23	3380	8330	12 (53)	79 (84)
Thailand	61	2000	6320	32 (53)	179 (79)
Pakistan	138	440	1860	17 (12)	62 (31)
Iran	64	1680	5910	27 (42)	136 (71)
Saudi Arabia	21	7230	11390	13 (61)	78 (87)
South Africa	43	3020	9160	17 (40)	202 (83)
Brazil	170	3580	7300	75 (44)	641 (83)
Argentina**	37	7460	12050	31 (84)	314 (97)
Venezuela	24	4310	5740	13 (56)	87 (86)
Colombia	42	2020	6060	19 (45)	136 (83)
Mexico	98	5070	8790	68 (69)	624 (93)
Turkey	65	3100	7030	45 (69)	265 (85)
Poland	39	4190	9000	34 (86)	206 (95)
Ukraine	50	700	3700	12 (23)	44 (45)
Russia	146	1660	8010	68 (47)	436 (79)
Totals	3632	xx	xx	1059 (29)	***6305 (67)

Source: Myers, N., J. Kent. "The New Consumers: The Influence of Affluence on the Environment." *Proceedings of the National Academy of Sciences* (USA) 100 (2003), 4963–4968.

*Equates to household consumption.
**Argentina's total will have declined somewhat by today.
***This total approaches that of the United States, with $6.7 trillion.

The 20 New-Consumer Countries

In 14 of the 20 countries, new consumers make up 12–56% of the population, and in the other 6 countries they account for 61–96%. Virtually all the 20 countries have featured strong economic growth for most if not all of the past 10 years, and in a few instances for 20 years. More importantly, many of them feature even stronger growth of consumption on the part of the most affluent sectors of their populations, these being the sectors that feature the new consumers. Asia in particular features 10 of the 20 new consumer countries, and their new-consumer numbers, 677 million in 2000, amounted to two-thirds of the worldwide total, making this the center of gravity for the new-consumer phenomenon.

Certain other populous countries could make the list through the population criterion: Vietnam, Bangladesh, Egypt, Ethiopia, Nigeria, and Peru have 25 or more million people (two of them more than 100 million), but they are not economically advanced enough to have many new consumers. Nigeria, for instance, had 134 million people in 2003 but a per-capita GNI of only around PPP$800, so it is likely to have only a few million new consumers. India makes the list even though its per-capita GNI was low at around PPP$2500 in 2002. Its skewed income distribution means that the top 10% enjoy incomes three to four times as much as the national average. Moreover, its huge population means that if only 5% were to qualify as new consumers, that would still be well over 50 million, hence significant for the overall total of new consumers. Similarly, Indonesia had a low-ish per-capita GNI of around PPP$3000 in 2002, but its population of 220 million features a skewedness of income distribution akin to India's, meaning the country must contain a good number of new consumers. By contrast, if a country with only 19 million people were to feature 50% of them as new consumers, that would make marginal difference to the 20 countries' total.

Several fairly affluent countries, such as Chile, Czech Republic, Slovakia, and Hungary, are omitted because they have small populations, hence they have limited scope to generate new consumers. Taiwan has 23 million people and its per-capita GNI/PPP is likely to match that of the most affluent new-consumer countries, but for political reasons (mainland China considers Taiwan as one of its provinces, not a separate country), its economic data are not readily available in World Bank or United Nations documents, so it too falls off the list. A rough reckoning suggests that all these eleven countries would have no more than around 150 million new consumers, so they would not make much difference to the grand total for the 20 countries with their 1.1 billion new consumers (for a qualifier as concerns four exceptionally affluent new consumer countries, South Korea, Mexico, Turkey, and Poland, see appendix B).

The new consumers have a far-reaching impact on economic activities nationwide, and hence on environmental repercussions (with, in turn, their own economic costs). In India, for example, new consumers accounted for only one-seventh of the year 2000 population but more than two-fifths of the country's purchasing power. In the major sector of transportation, especially cars, they accounted in the late 1990s for 85% of citizens' spending on getting from here to there. Their per-capita energy consumption was causing CO_2 emissions fifteen times greater than those of the rest of India's population.[17] In Russia, half of all consumer goods are bought by the affluent elite who comprise one-fifth of the population.[18] Many of these Russian purchases are household appliances powered by electricity, which is usually generated by fossil fuels with their CO_2 emissions.

The Special Case of China

China is the biggie in the new consumers arena, with almost 30% of all new consumers. To cater to them, the government is set on building up its car fleet from only eight million in 2000 (no more than Chicago's) to one of the biggest fleets in the world, and doing so in next to no time. As early as 2010 the cars total could surpass 40 million, or one-quarter as many as in the United States today (for details, see chapter II). What, you might say, could China become number two in cars in a few decades' time? Well, who would have bet in 1990 that within ten years China would become the world's foremost consumer of meat, grain, steel, and coal? Unfortunately there is another side to the cars explosion: they are the fastest growing source of CO_2 emissions.

Some basic statistics: The country supports 20% of the world's population on 7% of the world's arable land, and with 6% of the world's freshwater and 4% of the world's forests.[19] Although China's territory is almost exactly the same size as the United States', only one-seventh is cropland by contrast with one-fifth.

In addition to cars, China has developed a hearty appetite for meat. During the 1990s it nearly doubled its meat intake, to become the world leader in meat consumption, 85% more than the second biggest carnivore country, the United States. Increasingly, much of China's meat is raised on grain, which aggravates pressure on limited stocks of irrigation water for grainlands as well as increased demand for grain supplies from international markets. To produce 1 metric ton (tonne) of grain can take 1000 tonnes of water. Several regions of China experience water shortages already, accentuated in part by the surging demand for grain. The North China Plain features two-fifths of the country's population and two-thirds of its croplands but only one-fifth of its surface water. Overpumping of the region's aquifers have been causing water levels to decline by a whole meter or more per year.

China's future could be surprising in still other ways. If the country can maintain its economic surge of the last two decades, it could become the world's biggest PPP economy by 2020, a time less distant from now than the first cracks in the Soviet monolith are behind us. This would offer scope for fast-climbing numbers of new consumers, perhaps a doubling of the 2000 total as soon as 2010. Given the country's economic globalization and the spread of Western lifestyles, a potential doubling of its new consumers within the present decade presents a major challenge when it is linked with shortages of grain and water, plus loss of cropland for urbanization, transport networks, and the lengthy like (for details, see chapter V). The prospect is further difficult in terms of CO_2 emissions, which in 2001 placed China second to the United States with around half as much CO_2 output even though per capita they produced only one-eighth as much.[20]

China is no longer a sleeping giant, it is awake and roaring. Are we listening? After all, China is set to become a front-rank player in both the global economic and environmental arenas, rivaled only by the United States. And who's hearkening to the even bigger roar of one billion new consumers with their unprecedented potential to reconfigure both the world's economies and its environments?

These prognostications require a caveat as concerns projections. Projections are simply that—extensions of recent trends. They can swiftly become misleading. (For instance, in the 1970s California's population was growing by 3% per year through immigration of fellow Americans; a projection would have suggested that eventually all Americans would be living there.) The United Nations and the World Bank regularly publish projections as far ahead as 2010 and even 2020 (occasionally they peer into the remote future of 2050). But the world is subject to all manner of changes of direction, even fundamental shifts in economic and political spheres, notably financial meltdowns and government ousters as well as environmental break points ("threshold effects" of degradation). Then there are "bolts from the blue" such as SARS with its setback to China's economy—though it will make scant difference to the long-term trajectory of China's success story.

It is hard to anticipate what the world will look like in ten years' time, let alone twice as far ahead. Recall how much the world has altered since 1980. So we should be a tad wary of, for example, a projection proposing that China will become the biggest economic power by 2020. Even discounting shocks to economic and political systems, we must bear in mind too that an economy does not generally expand in linear fashion. As it grows, it moves on from a primarily agricultural entity to one that is basically industrial, then an economy characterized by services. A mature economy begins to act like a sedate limousine rather than a high-octane sports car. While becoming more advanced, its growth rate can slacken by at least half. It could be questionable, then, that China will maintain a 7% growth as far ahead as 2020. Nonetheless a projection can be illuminating provided there is clear recognition of its limitations.

Overconsumption and Sustainable Consumption

The emergence of the new consumers could serve as a sharp reminder to the long-rich countries that consumption patterns will change, whether by choice or by compulsion. Environmental forces are becoming ever more forceful. There have been numerous statements along these lines by the U.S. National Academy of Sciences, the Union of Concerned Scientists, the InterAcademy Panel, and other professional bodies reflecting top-flight scientific opinion around the world; and they have been backed by parallel statements on the part of 2500 leading economists and Nobel Prize winners.[21] As we shall see in chapter II, cars are the fastest growing source of carbon dioxide emissions that cause half of global warming processes. As we shall see in chapter III, much of the new consumers' appetite for meat lies with meat raised in part on grain, and this new pressure on grain supplies is precipitating shortages that drive up grain prices worldwide—to the extent that Americans may soon notice the change at their supermarket checkouts. There may be further grain shortfalls brought on by global warming; unusually high temperatures and drought triggered a reduced grain harvest in Europe during 2003, with markedly increased prices for bread and other grain-based products. Global warming will levy the highest costs of all, with major setbacks to our economies—and if we eventually decide we don't want global warming and we take the measures necessary to reverse today's climate trends, we may find we need centuries to do the job.

To reinforce the point: all the many goods and services supplied by the environment—water, soils, genetic resources, watersheds, and even climate itself—have been calculated by cold-eyed economists to be worth virtually as much in dollar terms as all the goods and services supplied by our conventional economic activities. Thus we undercut our material well-being when we cause environmental goods and services to be degraded and otherwise depleted. In fact we are overexploiting our natural-resource base at a rate one-fifth more than it can renew itself. In short, environmental problems are economic problems, and they are costing us with every passing day.[22]

On top of all this, consumers may come to recognize that the good life does not reside in piling up ever-more goodies, and that the best things in life are not things. Could the time be coming for us to move on from "More is better" to "Enough is best"? Consider too how much consumption is excessive because it is simply wasteful. The United States loses at least $1 trillion of its $10 trillion economy each year on wasted energy, metals, wood, soil, water, and fiber, including the cost of moving them around.[23] Then there is the pollution problem. Almost all cars, that badge of consumerdom, are highly polluting, and large cars—much sought after by new consumers—are disproportionately polluting. A consumption revolution toward sustainable consumption could eventually rank as one of the most seismic shifts in personal outlooks and community values since we came out of our caves. As the Chinese would put it, we have interesting times ahead.

In addition to environmental impacts of overconsumption and misconsumption, there are equity considerations. This book hardly considers the 1.2 billion people in absolute poverty, that is those with income of less than $1 per day, nor the further 1.6 billion people with income of less than $2 per day, all of them in dire need of increasing their consumption. While their plight deserves to be addressed just as urgently and vigorously as that of the new consumers, it belongs only marginally in this book. Some focus will be directed, however, at the notion that overconsumption by the affluent can sometimes lead to underconsumption by the poor. As we have noted, eating high on the food chain, as is the case with virtually all new consumers, can lead to greatly increased consumption of grain via livestock, pushing up grain prices for all citizens in international markets and eventually placing grain imports beyond the reach of impoverished communities in Sub-Saharan Africa and the Indian subcontinent.

What, conversely, is "sustainable consumption"? To be technical, it can be defined as "the use of goods and services which respond to basic needs and bring a better quality of life while minimizing the use of natural resources and toxic materials as well as the emissions of wastes and pollutants over the lifecycle of goods and services so as not to jeopardize the needs of future generations" (phew!).[24] Or, more briefly, sustainable consumption amounts to the use of materials and energy that (a) enhances present-day's quality of life and (b) will not generate protests from our grandchildren that we have cut the environmental ground from under their feet. Consumption is fine, and more consumption is better, *provided* we do it in a fashion that means we can do it forever, plus a day to be on the safe side.

This book lays out salient aspects of the new-consumers phenomenon. Chapter II deals with one of the main manifestations of richer lifestyles, cars, while chapter III does the same with another manifestation, meat. Chapter IV reviews a further "resource linkage," that of household electricity; it also considers an overall assessment of all resource linkages in the form of "ecological footprints," and it concludes with a look at the impacts of population growth. In Chapters V and VI we consider the two countries with the largest numbers of new consumers, both present and prospective, viz China and India. Chapter VII touches base with the other 18 new-consumer countries, drawing out certain common themes. In two final chapters we ask again what is meant by "sustainable consumption," addressing the challenge in all countries of the world.

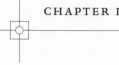

CHAPTER II

Cars: Driving Us Backwards

CARS SUPPLY a highly convenient mode of traveling from here to there. In emphatic addition, they are widely viewed as symbols of economic advancement as well as social status. They have long been sold for their image impact as much as their engine size. Not surprisingly, they are much sought after by the new consumers, who comprise virtually the entire markets for cars in most of the 20 new-consumer countries. At the same time, cars epitomize the many linkages between consumption and environment. They are expected to make up the fastest growing sector of energy use as far ahead as 2025, with all that implies for fossil fuels and pollution, especially CO_2 emissions.[1]

Car Numbers

The new consumers were driving 125 million cars in 2000, up from 63 million in 1990 and predicted to reach at least 245 million in 2010. By the 1980s when Brazil, Mexico, Malaysia, and several others of the more affluent new-consumer countries attained the income levels enjoyed by France, Germany, and Italy in the 1950s, cars amounted to more than 50 per 1000 people, twice as many as in the European countries of the 1950s.[2] They thus reflected the unusual affluence of the new consumers.

In addition, the new consumers' car fleets have been expanding more rapidly than national economies. During 1990–2000 South Korea's economy grew by almost three-quarters but its car fleet tripled.[3] As a further reflection of the surging purchasing power of the new consumers, Thailand has one of the developing world's highest per-capita number of luxury cars, while China is the biggest market outside Germany for Mercedes cars. A similar story applies in Brazil, Mexico, Turkey, and Poland.[4]

The leading car owner of the 20 countries in 2000 was Brazil with 23 million, followed by Russia with 20 million. Despite its total, Russia, with almost twice as many people as Germany, has been featuring only one-quarter as many new car sales as in Germany,[5] even though the three years 1998–2000 saw Russia's car numbers increase by 30%.[6] The next biggest cars countries were Mexico with 10.5 million and Poland with 10 million, followed by South Korea with 8.5 million and China with 8 million. The global car fleet totalled 560 million, of which the new consumer countries' share was almost one in five—meaning too that the new consumers total was three-quarters that of the United States. Pakistan still had only 5 cars per 1000 of population, India 6 and China 7, whereas Russia and Argentina had 140, Malaysia and South Korea 180, and Poland 260 (the United States 620, if we include sport-utility vehicles which make up every fifth new "car"; see table II.1).[7]

What counts most of all is the number of cars per 1000 new consumers. In this ranking Ukraine scored highest with 458 cars, even though new consumers made up less than every fourth of Ukraine's citizens. Offsetting this remarkable finding was the fact that a good share of the country's cars were old. Ranked second according to this "per 1000" criterion was Malaysia with 350, followed by Brazil with 314, and Russia with 300. Indonesia had only 48, India 46, and Philippines and China less than 30 each.

Several countries recorded exceptional growth in car numbers during the 1990s. China's fleet grew by 400%, from 1.6 million to 8 million (still only half as many as in Greater Los Angeles); India's by 205%, from 2 million to 6.1 million (still fewer than in Greater Chicago);

Colombia's by 217% from 0.6 million to 1.9 million; and South Korea's by 305% from 2.1 million to 8.5 million. By contrast, the United States' total grew by only 15% from 152 million to 175 million, largely because the country was nearing "car saturation"—the entire U.S. population could fit into cars with nobody in the back seats.[8]

These ultrarapid growth rates could serve as a portent of the potential surge in car numbers that could characterize the other new-consumer countries as their affluent communities keep on expanding their numbers and their wealth.[9] With its fast-growing economy and faster-growing middle class, China seems set to expand its car fleet

TABLE II.1: **The New Consumers' Cars in 1990 and 2000**

Country	1990, millions	2000, millions	Cars per 1000 new consumers	% change 1990–2000
China	1.6	8.0	26	400
India	2.0	6.1	46	205
South Korea	2.1	8.5	189	305
Philippines	0.4	0.8	24	100
Indonesia	1.3	3.0	48	131
Malaysia	1.8	4.2	350	133
Thailand	0.8	1.9	59	138
Pakistan	0.5	0.7	41	40
Iran	1.4	2.1	78	50
Saudi Arabia	1.6	1.9	146	19
South Africa	3.4	4.1	241	21
Brazil	11.8	23.2	314	97
Argentina	4.4	5.5	177	25
Venezuela	1.5	1.8	139	20
Colombia	0.6	1.9	100	217
Mexico	6.8	10.5	154	54
Turkey	1.9	4.5	100	137
Poland	5.3	10.1	297	91
Ukraine	3.3	5.5	458	67
Russia	10.1	20.4	300	102
Totals	63	125	118	102
% of world	13	22	xx	69
USA	152	*175	xx	15
World	478	560	xx	17

Source: Author calculations based on World Bank, World Development Indicators 2003 Database (http://www.world-bank.org/data/wdi2003/index.htm).

*Including SUVs.

with unprecedented speed—in fact this is a major government priority. Car production soared eightfold during the 1990s. If China maintains an annual per-capita economic growth rate of just 7%, rather than the 10% of the 1990s, together with an 18% annual growth rate in car numbers, its fleet of 8 million in 2000 could increase fivefold as early as 2010. The country would then have 42 million cars, almost as many as Germany today. This would be 70 cars per 1000 new consumers, though still far below the 620 per 1000 Americans today. Given the additional new consumers expected to come on stream and their increased affluence as compared with today's new consumers, the annual growth rate in China's car numbers could conceivably be even higher. Looking still further ahead and supposing that China becomes the world's leading economy by 2020 (see chapter V), the cars total by then could readily exceed 170 million.[10] All this depends of course on recent trends being maintained for a good many years ahead; recall chapter I's caveat that projections are not forecasts, still less are they predictions.

Much the same pattern will apply to India during the current decade. With a projected per-capita economic growth rate of 6% per year and a growth in car numbers, as in the 1990s, of 12% per year, the cars total could well rise from 6 million in 2000 to 19 million in 2010, though still only 76 cars per 1000 new consumers.[11] In Mexico the number of motor vehicles per 1000 new consumers stood at one-quarter of the U.S. level in 2000 and is expected to jump to half during the present decade.

Next, consider car numbers relative to per-capita income growth, based on trends in China, India, South Korea, and Malaysia, plus certain Latin American countries (trends that in turn have followed those of Europe and even the United States). The "GNI intensity of car ownership" is increasing most in Asia. In several countries a doubling of GNI is accompanied by way more than a doubling of car numbers, after the manner of Japan which, during the period 1965–75 when its per-capita GDP doubled, the per-capita number of cars more than quadrupled.[12]

In short, the car culture is hitting high gear in the new-consumer countries. During the 1990s the 10 Asian countries' fleets climbed by 176% to 37 million cars, while the five Latin American countries' fleets grew by 71% to reach 43 million. Car numbers in Turkey and the three Eastern European countries grew by 97% to reach 41 million. South Africa's fleet grew by only 21% to reach a mere 4.1 million.[13]

As for the future, recall that the 20 new-consumer countries registered an aggregate 100% increase in car numbers during the 1990s, for an average annual rate of 7%. Some, notably China, India, South Korea, and Colombia have posted a recent annual car growth rate of 12–20%, largely due to the disproportionately fast growth of per-capita incomes among their middle classes.[14] Now consider the period 2000–2010 and allow for growth in the numbers of people joining the middle classes, together with their relatively growing wealth, also the headlong "motorization" planned for China and India. All this could well make the 2010 total still higher. Suppose that all 20 new-consumer countries register an average annual increase in car numbers of 7%, a conservative estimate. This will mean a total of around 245 million cars in 2010, almost double the total in 2000.

Environmental Problems

Cars rank among the most environmentally harmful of all types of consumption. They cause much pollution, whether in the form of urban smog, acid rain, or global warming. The main pollutants are suspended particulates, sulphur dioxide, and nitrogen oxides as well as CO_2. The first of these presents the biggest direct threat to human health, the second and third cause acid rain, and the fourth contributes half of global warming processes. Motor vehicles, of which cars make up three-quarters, are by far the fastest growing and ostensibly the most intractable source of CO_2 emissions, emitting one-fifth of energy-related emissions worldwide and three-quarters of transport-related emissions.[15] On top of all this, cars generate many local economic and social costs, notably road congestion, traffic delays, accidents, and costly land use.[16]

Traffic congestion is not just a developed-country problem. In some localities of developing countries, there are already too many cars for the roads. In Bangkok there are long periods every day when traffic moves at an average speed (if that is the right word) of 3 kilometers per hour, equal to strolling pace, while cars spend an average of forty-four days per year stuck in traffic. Just these problems cost at least $2.3 billion (possibly several times more) in lost worker productivity per year, plus $1.6 billion of energy wasted in idling car engines.[17] One million respiratory infections each year are linked to air pollution, and cancer rates are three times higher than in other parts of Thailand.[18] Fortunately, and despite a growing vehicle population, Bangkok's air has become somewhat cleaner now that leaded gasoline has been banned and all new cars have to meet European emission standards.

Consider also the case of India, where the emergent car culture is supplying many benefits to the few who own cars and large costs to those who do not. Cars cause more than half of the air pollution in Mumbai (formerly Bombay) and New Delhi.[19] True, for every car in India there are two two- and three-wheeler vehicles, but the point stands. In New Delhi, motor vehicles have caused the city to rank as one of the most polluted cities in the world, and an average of 7500 people have been dying from air pollutants each year while 1.2 million people have needed medical treatment. The annual health costs of air pollution in 36 Indian cities have been estimated for the mid-1990s at between $500 million and $2.1 billion.[20] Fortunately there have been major efforts to improve air quality in New Delhi, as too in Beijing and Mexico City.[21]

Air pollution from motor vehicles is a pronounced problem in many other new-consumer countries. In China, as much as 60% of air pollution stems from vehicle emissions, mainly from cars.[22] It has been causing at least 175,000 deaths per year, possibly several times more, plus nearly two million documented cases of chronic bronchitis. In Sao Paulo, 90% of smog stems from motor vehicle emissions, again mainly from cars (in reaction to which, the city government requires that motorists leave their cars at home one day a week).[23] Mexico City, with its 20 million inhabitants and two-fifths of the country's cars, is one of the world's most polluted cities.[24] Just airborne particulates (not counting other pollutants) were killing 6400 of the city's people a year in the mid-1990s,[25] while the mortality and morbidity impacts of all air pollution were levying annual costs of over $1 billion, worth $60 per resident.[26] The better news is that lead concentrations in Mexico City have been almost entirely eliminated.[27] Total health costs from particulates alone in all developing world cities, albeit from factories and other sources as well as cars, amounted to almost $100 billion in 1995.[28] As for a transition country, the average car in Poland is ten years old and far more polluting than new cars, while only a little more than one-quarter feature catalytic converters.

Traffic congestion is already acute and growing rapidly worse in a good number of other cities in new-consumer countries. In Manila, for instance, vehicles travel at an average of only 11 kilometers per hour, equivalent to jogging speed.[29] As far back as 1994, congestion costs amounted to $293 million in Hong Kong, $154 million in Seoul, and $68 million in each of Jakarta and Kuala Lumpur.[30]

The most important pollutant in the long run is CO_2, with its major contribution to global warming. Most cars emit their own weight in CO_2 each year, and in some new-consumer countries at least one-eighth of emissions may stem from cars.[31] Over the next 20 years, CO_2 emissions in developing countries are expected to grow by three-quarters, almost three times faster than in developed countries.[32] Without measures to restrict CO_2 emissions, the new consumers' cars in 2010 will contribute a sizeable share of all CO_2 emissions worldwide.

There are still further costs of cars. In India the fast-growing cars total requires many more rural roads and other infrastructure for a country where cropland is already scarce. In China the position is becoming equally acute and could eventually mean the paving over of a sizeable proportion of the country's croplands.[33]

If traffic pollution were a disease, huge international funds and other resources would be mobilized to tackle it. And if a runaway car culture were recognized as a major roadblock (so to speak) on the way to sustainable consumption, whether in economic, environmental, or social terms, there would surely be far greater efforts to contain the surge in car numbers. It is entirely possible (see below) even if little practiced.

The Cars Phenomenon in Developed Countries

The new-consumer countries might consider the "cars experience" in developed countries, and ponder whether they want to follow the same route into their future. They might also ask whether the experience does not cause developed countries to rank, in this respect at least, as overdeveloped or misdeveloped countries. In 1900 the main mode of transport in London was the horse-drawn carriage. Over the past century while London has grappled with the transition from travel by horse to travel by car, it has invested billions of pounds in its road networks—only to end up with car travel that is often no faster than by horse.

Still more to the point is the United States' experience, a country where the car is king (or tyrant). With less than 5% of the world's population, Americans consume 43% of the world's gasoline, making the country a gasoline junkie.[34] For every five cars added to the U.S. fleet, an area the size of a football field is covered with asphalt ("the land's last crop").[35] Road congestion costs the U.S. economy $80 billion per year, including 4.5 billion hours of lost work time and 6.8 billion gallons of wasted gasoline.[36] Probably most important of all, the transportation sector, primarily made up of cars and heavily reliant on oil, accounts for as many CO_2 emissions as all sources in all but a few countries.[37]

Oil imports made up two-fifths of U.S. consumption in 1985, soaring to almost two-thirds today. Sizeable amounts come from the Persian Gulf and other OPEC members. The imports in 2000 cost well over $100 billion, or as much as the country earns from its grain exports.[38] Despite all this, many Americans have taken to buying sport-utility vehicles (SUVs), surely the most conspicuous form of consumption. SUV sales have surged from 2% of motor vehicles in 1985 to 25% in 2001, yet only one in every 20 SUVs is used in off-road conditions, with the other 19 consuming excessive amounts of gasoline.[39] Fortunately, one of the more popular new cars in 2002 came from the other end of the size spectrum, the Mini, being a British model that's among the smallest on the road. This remarkable shift in public taste notwithstanding, the new consumers might well ask: Is this the sort of car culture we want to aim for? Are traffic jams, smog clouds, and universal asphalt to be viewed as an ultimate badge of prosperity?

Since the late 1980s, U.S. car fuel efficiency has not improved at all. It could have leaped ahead if it had developed fuel-efficient cars such as the Toyota Prius and the Honda Insight. The average new American car might be the highest expression of the Iron Age, but its 35 kilometers per gallon matches a 20-year low.[40] Switching to an SUV for one year wastes more energy than leaving a refrigerator door open for six years or leaving a bathroom light on for 30 years. Fortunately, the state government of California has proposed replacing all government SUVs.[41] At the same time, a number of Hollywood stars and other trendsetters are leading the way toward enlightenment by driving the latest fuel-efficient vehicles.

A piece of potentially better news is that raising U.S. car efficiency to 65 kilometers per gallon (well within manufacturers' capabilities) would save more oil than America's Persian Gulf imports, plus drilling in offshore California and the Arctic National Wildlife Refuge, all of which need to be boosted according to President Bush. Even better, fuel efficiency could one day be tripled. Amory Lovins, the American energy expert, has designed a "hypercar," largely made of advanced polymer composites and weighing only one-third as much as a conventional car. Thanks to these efficiencies and a hybrid-electric drive, it could eventually travel as much as 300 kilometers off a single gallon. It will be 95% less polluting, and almost entirely recyclable.[42]

A Better Road Ahead

Now for the better news. There are plenty of ways for the new consumers to avoid some of the problems of a car culture run amok.[43] One such breakthrough is demonstrated by the city of Curitiba in southeastern Brazil. With 2.6 million people, it is located in the heart of a region as affluent as southern Europe and hence featuring a lot of new consumers. Instead of adapting the city and its people to roads, Curitiba works the other way round. The key lies with almost 2000 buses carrying some 200 passengers each along 1100 kilometers of express-lane routes. The bus network has been established at a cost ten times less than for a surface train. Moreover, new bus lanes can be installed within a few months instead of the several years needed for a surface train.

The buses make daily trips equivalent to nine times around the world. They carry three-quarters of the city's commuters, 1.9 million passengers each weekday, at a cost of less than half a U.S. dollar per ride. The system has cut the number of car drivers by one-quarter—significant for a city with half a million cars and with the highest rate of car ownership in Brazil except for Brasilia. Yet there are next to no traffic snarl-ups, thanks to citizens' benign neglect of their cars. In fact Curitiba claims the lowest rate of car drivership in Brazil, as well as the cleanest urban air. During the two decades 1976–95 bus ridership increased by almost half, while during the same period every other Brazilian city and most cities elsewhere in the world experienced significant declines in bus ridership. Today two-thirds of all trips are made by bus, whereas in other Brazilian cities only one-third are. During the past quarter century, Curitiba's car traffic has declined by almost one-third even while the population has doubled.[44]

A similar breakthrough is underway in Colombia's capital city, Bogota, with its seven million people, many of them new consumers. Cars have been accounting for more than 70% of trips shorter than 3 kilometers. In late 2000 the mayor launched a plan to improve both road transportation and air quality in Latin America's third most polluted city. Already the plan has installed a network of four-lane roads for buses, increasing the average bus speed from 10 to 25 kilometers per hour. The plan has also instituted a system of partially car-free days, based on the last number of the license plate, thus taking two-fifths of cars off the road during peak travel times. It has also extended bicycle tracks to nearly 200 kilometers. Plus there is to be a doubling of downtown parking prices and a 20% tax on gasoline. All this has reduced round-trip commuting times by up to one hour, and it has slashed traffic accidents by almost one-third.[45]

Today there are bus-based rapid-transit systems not only in Curitiba, Bogota, and a few other developing-country cities, but also in developed-country counterparts such as Ottawa, Pittsburgh, and Nagoya. By providing both high capacity and high speed, such systems attract more riders and provide better service than do conventional bus systems.[46]

Bogota's emphasis on bicycles recalls Europe's recent experience, where car use in certain cities has actually been declining as railroads and buses have linked up with bike routes. In Sweden roughly 12% of all trips are by bike and 10% by public transit, while almost 40% are on foot and only 36% are by car. In several Dutch cities bicycles account for up to half of all trips. In Copenhagen one-third of the population commutes to work by bike, and the city will soon provide 3000 bicycles for free use. In Tokyo 90% of workers commute by rail, and 30% reach their local rail station by bike.[47]

These various forms of infrastructure show that affluence need not lead to overloading of roads. Residents of Tokyo and Singapore drive cars an average of one-half less than people in Seoul, Manila, Jakarta, Kuala Lumpur, and Bangkok, even though they are several times wealthier. The more affluent cities have invested in infrastructure for noncar transportation, thus providing better travel options.[48] China's most prosperous city, Shanghai, has put $10 billion into a rapid-transit system, including the first line of its new subway system. It has also followed Singapore's example of adopting strong disincentives for car ownership, including registration limits and high taxes on large vehicles.[49]

Let us bear in mind too the experience of the richest part of the country where the car is king, namely Manhattan in New York. Many people do not own a car at all because of the high cost of garaging the thing. The buses and subway system are good enough for the working week, and if at the weekend citizens want to go off and enjoy the countryside or visit friends in a neighboring city, they simply hire a car. Better than having an expensive car for one hour's use per day and then leaving the machine to sit idle and depreciate for the other twenty-three hours.

Still another way to tame the car is through fuel taxes. Countries with high taxes tend to use cars least. In Germany the tax component of gasoline prices is 78%, in Britain it is 76%, and in Japan 53%, by contrast with the United States' 29%.[50] Another way lies with road pricing. Singapore uses electronic smart cards to charge people for driving downtown during peak hours. Melbourne uses tolls on its Citilink central freeways, with prices varying according to traffic density. Other European cities with road pricing schemes include London, Oslo, Rotterdam, Barcelona, Zurich, Rome, and Stockholm.[51] Taken together, these transportation measures can reduce car use by anywhere between 35% and 60%.[52]

There is scope too for alternative fuels. In Argentina, every tenth car—more than in any other country—runs on compressed natural gas. India requires the same fuel for all heavy vehicles in its major cities. Mexico uses tax policies to favor unleaded gasoline, low-sulfur diesel fuel, and reformulated gasoline, plus upgraded emission standards for new vehicles. Poland also uses the tax system to encourage unleaded gasoline and low-sulfur diesel fuel.[53]

A further strategy is simply to build cars that are more efficient and less polluting. Recall the hybrid or twin-fuel cars Toyota Prius and Honda Insight that can gain 100 kilometers per gallon of gasoline while emitting 40% less CO_2 than a gasoline-engine car of similar size.[54] Similar hybrids are due for early production by General Motors, Ford, and Daimler-Chrysler. Even more revolutionary are the fuel-cell cars scheduled by Mercedes-Benz, Honda, Toyota, and Nissan. These will run on hydrogen fuel generated through renewable energy, the sole tailpipe emission being water vapor.[55] The market for clean vehicles is projected to zoom from $2 billion in 2000 to $48 billion by 2010.[56] Six of the world's smoggiest cities—including such new-consumer cities as Sao Paulo, Beijing, Shanghai, New Delhi, and Mexico City—are to benefit from fuel-cell powered buses, and cars must surely follow.

Meantime the European Automobile Manufacturers Association has voluntarily committed its members to increasing auto fuel efficiency to 65 kilometers per gallon by 2008, while Japan aims for 56 kilometers by 2010. In the United States, by contrast, the fuel-economy standard for new cars is less than 40 kilometers per gallon, the second-worst figure in 20 years, and the standard keeps on declining as more SUVs come on the market.[57] In addition, European car makers must reduce their CO_2 emissions by 22%, whereas U.S. makers face no such requirement.[58]

Finally, the South Korean car manufacturer KIA has come up with an innovative response. It has launched a campaign in Britain urging purchasers of its cars not to use them for short journeys, and by way of encouragement has provided a mountain bike with every new car sold.[59]

Conclusion

Cars represent the ultimate of "You've made it." As any glossy magazine's ads emphasize, they spell prestige, power, and sex. Hence they are avidly sought after by the new consumers. They bring much convenient travel too, but also traffic snarl-ups, and road rage. And—let's hear it again because it is so crucial to all our futures—cars are the fastest growing source of CO_2 emissions. Do we have to wait until sea levels are expanding right around the world before we expand our bus services?

If only we were a fraction so good at birth control for cars as for people.

CHAPTER III

Meat: Juicy Steaks and Hidden Costs

NEW CONSUMERS have an appetite for meat, ever more meat. Whereas their fellow citizens enjoy pork, beef, or poultry only once a week at best, the new consumers mostly eat it once a day at least. During the 1990s when the world's meat consumption grew by 30%, the new-consumer countries' consumption grew by twice as much, the bulk of the meat going down the throats of the new consumers.

This is fine in many respects. Ever since humans became humans a quarter of a million years ago, they have liked to eat meat as much as plants—provided they could get it, which wasn't often. This book's first author grew up on a semisubsistence farm in northern England, and I noticed that when there was a gathering of relatives and friends, they would eat as much meat as they could, and then some more. After people throughout history have developed a powerful taste for this protein-rich food, it is not surprising that the new consumers are bent on following suit. But the new consumers' pleasure in meat, implicitly too in the grain and water often required to supply livestock feed,[1] will hit hard at their countries' economies as well as their environments. Further afield, it could eventually impact on prices for American food shoppers.[2]

Until many developed-world citizens embarked on affluent lifestyles a century or so ago, meat was still a scarce item—a fact that lay

behind Italian, Spanish, and other cuisines which made a little meat go
a long way. Then as people became better off, they began to eat more
and more meat. Since 1950 and as the developed countries entered
economic boom times, they have generally seen meat consumption
grow twice as fast as population.[3] In the past decade, however, much
if not most of the surging demand for meat has been due to the emergence of the new consumers.

This latest trend is likely to continue. Of the world's 22 billion livestock (17 billion of them poultry) 13 billion are in new-consumer
countries (5.7 billion in China, by contrast with 2.2 billion in the United
States).[4] Whereas many developed-country people have become sated
with meat (consumption has recently declined a little in Europe), the
new-consumer countries have a long way to go. If the developing
world's appetite for meat grows as expected until it almost doubles
during 1997–2020, its livestock numbers could climb to 28 billion
animals. Most of these additional animals will be in new-consumer
countries.[5]

Consider China in particular. With 20% of the world's population,
the country accounts for 28% of the world's meat consumption. It
chomps its way through four-fifths more meat than the United States,
making it the world's largest carnivore country, even though an average Chinese person's meat consumption is no more than 50 kilograms
or so per year, way below an American's 122 kilograms (which is
almost twice his/or her weight).[6] During 1980–2000 China's meat consumption overall grew 4.5-fold and per person 3.5-fold. Of course the
50 kilograms per person average conceals the fact that the great bulk
of the increased meat is enjoyed by China's new consumers, while the
other one billion Chinese still view meat as an occasional treat.

Regrettably there is no way to figure out the precise share of meat
consumption's growth attributable to new consumers in individual
countries. Nor are data available on meat consumption for sectors of
national populations such as the richest one-fifth. All we can do is to
note anecdotal statements on leading meat-eating countries such as
China and Brazil. These suggest that since meat is somewhat of a high-
price item if not a luxury item, most of the recent increase in meat

consumption, surely three-quarters or even more, can be attributed to the new consumers even though in many countries they make up only one-third or less of their countries' populations. In Poland new consumer households consume four times as much meat as poorer households.[7] Other new consumer countries apart from China and Brazil are shifting to strongly meat-based diets. South Korea doubled its meat consumption during just the 1990s, while Philippines, Malaysia and Mexico achieved almost as much.[8] So great is the sociocultural shift that even some traditionally vegetarian communities of India have begun to eat meat. Overall, then, the soaring appetite for meat on the part of new consumers is a key factor in the recent expansion of the developing world's meat economy.

Concealed Costs of the Meat Economy

While most people enjoy a good juicy steak or a quick-fix hamburger, the new consumers should be aware that a meat diet has its costs apart from what they pay at the restaurant or the butcher's. The dietary revolution often leads to overloading of grainlands (see below) result ing in soil erosion and other forms of land degradation.[9] Livestock's demand for new pasturelands can serve to take over forests and wildlife habitats.[10] In addition, livestock can be environmentally costly in terms of greenhouse gases (GHGs). Cattle and other ruminants generate methane amounting to one-sixth of global emissions, a share that is likely to climb in response to expanding appetites for meat.[11] Then there are livestock wastes, which are widely implicated in waterway pollution, toxic algal blooms, and extensive fish kills; in the United States, livestock waste is 130 times greater than that from humans.[12] On top of all this are the problems that a high-fat and high-calorie meat can inflict on health. A steak a day overloads the arteries for life and even for early death.

The Grain Connection

In short, the new consumers should tuck into their steaks and hamburgers with gusto, provided—a big "provided"—they remember they can never do only one thing. Much meat is raised in part at least on grain, and stacks of feedlots are springing up in China, Philippines, Brazil, and most other new-consumer countries. Now that rangelands and other pasturelands are becoming widely exploited if not overexploited in much of the world, there will be increased emphasis on feedlots.[13] In many countries, indeed, feedlot production has become the fastest growing method for raising livestock.[14]

China now allocates almost one-quarter of its grain to livestock, and Brazil and Saudi Arabia more than one-half each. In nine of the 20 new-consumer countries, feed grain amounts to two-fifths or more of all grain consumed. These are huge shares for developing countries, though still behind the United States' two-thirds.[15] Moreover in Mexico the past two decades have seen the share of grain going to livestock climb rapidly to 41%.[16] One kilogram of feedlot beef can take 7 kilograms of grain, of pork 4 kilograms, and of poultry 2 kilograms,[17] which makes beef far more expensive than other meats and an item purchased almost entirely by the new consumers. The grain connection means that feedlot meat is a very inefficient way for consumers to get their protein. One hectare of grain produces five times more direct protein than a hectare indirectly devoted to meat. The beef in a burger can represent enough wheat to produce five loaves of bread.

Unaware of it as they may be, the new consumers' preference for meat will have a profound impact on those countries that depend for much of their grain upon imports. In Colombia, imports amount to roughly one-half all grain consumption; in Venezuela, two thirds; and in South Korea, Malaysia, and Saudi Arabia, three-quarters. Of the 20 countries, 9 import one-fifth or more of their grain, and another six import significant amounts (by contrast, China, India, and Pakistan import little if any of their grain as yet, while Argentina and Thailand are sizeable exporters). Similarly, Philippines imports 27% of its grain, yet it assigns a similar share of its grain to livestock; Brazil 21% and 54%.[18] These imports put pressure on international grain markets, to the detriment of poor countries that can hardly afford rising prices. Worse, the added pressure arises at a time when global grain harvests are no longer keeping up with demand. In the three years 2000–2002 the harvests fell far short of consumption, dropping grain reserves to their lowest level in three decades. In response, prices for both wheat and corn climbed by roughly 30%.[19] Meantime the world's population grows by more than 80 million people a year, and world grain demand by roughly 16 million tonnes a year.[20]

Overall the grain arithmetic is this. The global harvest is around 1900 million tonnes per year, of which 340 million tonnes is grown in each of China and the United States, and almost 200 million tonnes in India. Grain traded worldwide amounts to just short of 300 million tonnes per year, of which 90 million tonnes comes from the United States, being sold or donated to more than 100 countries that are adequately fed courtesy of Uncle Sam. So a good number of countries and as many as one billion people could find themselves sorely pressed in tightening grain markets. The 2003 global grain harvest fell short of consumption by 93 million tonnes (contrast 16 million tonnes in 2001), dropping grain stocks to the lowest level in 30 years.[21]

Note China again. It diverts almost one-quarter of its grain to livestock, an amount twice as much as in 1980. If this trend continues, and if population growth of eight million people per year requires yet more grain as direct human food, China could depend on grain imports for fully one-tenth of its total consumption, possibly twice as much, thereby becoming the world's number one importer by a long way.[22] India is another country that neither exports nor imports much grain, yet by 2020 it could be facing a grain shortfall of one-quarter of its expected consumption, probably making it the world's second biggest importer. This means that China and India alone would be seeking almost three times more grain than the United States exports today—possibly more and earlier.[23]

Apart from the economics of grain imports, there is a social aspect to meat appetites. All that grain going to livestock means less going to hungry people in the 20 countries.[24] A person living on a vegetarian diet needs 200 kilograms of grain per year. A malnourished person is generally falling short by at least 40 kilograms. Just one-tenth of the 85 million tonnes of grain thát China fed to its livestock in 2000, 8.5

million tonnes, could have more than made up the diets of its malnourished total of 120 million people, being almost every tenth person in the country. In Philippines every fifth person is malnourished,
yet in 2000 the country fed 4 million tonnes of grain to its livestock,
one-tenth of which would help out its 17 million hungry people.
Other major grain importers and major meat eaters include Brazil
with 17 million people malnourished, every tenth person; Colombia
with 5.6 million, every eighth person; and Venezuela with almost 5
million, every fifth person.[25] (See table III.1.)

Note in particular the international role of the United States. It
exports one-quarter of its grain harvest and supplies almost one-third

TABLE III.1. **Meat and Grain in 2000**

Country	Meat, million tonnes	Grain, million tonnes	Food grain, million tonnes	Feed grain, million tonnes (and % of total grain)	Meat, kgs per capita	Food grain, % kgs per capita increase 1990–2000	Feed grain % kgs per capita increase 1990–2000	Grain imports as % of total grain	Under-nourished millions
China	64.3	366	243	85 (23)	50	-9	20	3	119
India	4.6	179	160	2 (1)	5	2	0	<0.1	233
South Korea	2.2	17	8	8 (44)	46	-7	36	75	1
Philippines	2.0	16	10	4 (28)	27	-6	14	27	17
Indonesia	1.7	52	43	2 (4)	8	11	50	14	12
Malaysia	1.1	6	3	3 (41)	51	19	22	76	0.4
Thailand	1.5	15	8	5 (34)	24	11	11	9	12
Pakistan	1.8	26	22	1 (4)	12	5	33	4	26
Iran	1.5	22	13	7 (32)	22	3	10	44	4
Saudi Arabia	1.0	10	3	6 (65)	46	-7	84	78	1
South Africa	1.7	14	8	4 (32)	39	-1	-4	14	n/a
Brazil	13.0	53	18	29 (54)	77	-3	44	21	17
Argentina	3.6	15	5	7 (44)	98	-1	28	1	0.4
Venezuela	1.0	4	3	1 (18)	42	-9	-31	68	5
Colombia	1.4	6	4	2 (30)	34	15	47	53	6
Mexico	5.5	41	18	17 (41)	56	1	8	36	5
Turkey	1.3	32	14	8 (25)	20	-6	3	9	2
Poland	2.7	25	6	14 (58)	70	6	-23	9	0.3
Ukraine	1.5	22	8	11 (50)	31	-12	-40	5	3
Russia	5.8	68	22	33 (48)	40	-6	-44	9	7
Totals	119	989	619	248 (25)	—	—	—	—	471.1
Share of world	52%	53%	65%	38%	—	—	—	—	56%
USA	35	255	32	169 (66)	122	5	1	3	—
Share of world	15%	14%	3%	36%	—	—	—	—	—
World	230	1870	948	659 (35)	38	-2	-11	—	840

Source: FAOSTAT Food Balance Sheets Database (http://apps.fao.org/page/collections?subset=nutrition).
Note: Food grain and feed grain do not equate to total grain, which include seed, processing, waste, etc.; n/a = not available.

of all grain exports,[26] but a large share of U.S. exports goes to feed live-stock rather than hungry people. At the same time, the U.S. govern-ment has long encouraged, via its foreign aid program, the expansion of feed-grain markets to absorb its grain exports.[27] At least four out of five of the world's hungry children live in countries with food sur-pluses, part of which is in the form of grain fed to animals for con-sumption by affluent consumers.

Finally, a quick look at the future. Between 1997 and 2020 the de-veloping world as a whole—of whose populations, almost three-quarters now reside in seventeen new-consumer countries—is expected to increase its demand for grain by 50%, for food grain by 39%, for feed grain by 85%, and for meat by 92%. It will thus account for around 86% of the increase in global demand for both grain and meat (see table III.2).[28]

The Water Connection

The "ecological footprint" of meat production is also deep and wide with respect to water. Increased grain harvests aggravate water short-ages. To produce one tonne of grain can take 1000 tonnes of water, sometimes a good deal more.[29] Alternatively stated, 1 kilogram of water equates to 1 liter, so 1 kilogram of grain can account for 1000

TABLE III.2. **Grain and Meat Demand 1997–2020**

	Grain supply 1997, million tonnes	Grain demand 2020, million tonnes	Increase 1997–2020, million tonnes (and % increase projected)	Meat supply 1997, million tonnes	Meat demand projected 2020, million tonnes	Increase 1997–2020, million tonnes (and % increase projected)
China	385	558	173 (45)	55	104	49 (89)
India	182	260	78 (43)	5	10	5 (100)
All developing countries	1118	1675	557 (50)	111	213	102 (92)
All developed countries	725	822	97 (13)	97	114	17 (18)
World	1843	2497	654 (36)	208	327	119 (57)

Sources: FAOSTAT Food Balance Sheets Database (http://apps.fao.org/page/collections?subset=nutrition); M. W. Rosegrant, M. S. Paisner, S. Meijer, and J. Witcover, *2020 Global Food Outlook* (Washington, D.C.: International Food Policy Research Institute, 2001).

liters, or as much as would fill five bath tubs. The water used to produce just a quarter-kilogram steak can equal the entire in-house water consumption of an American family for one day. An affluent American effectively consumes more than 1 tonne of grain per year, a huge four-fifths of it by eating grain-fed livestock products. A diet featuring meat most days of the week requires twice as much water to produce the food as an average developing-country diet; and in countries where irrigation water is used with scant efficiency, a new consumer may use three times as much water.[30] Conversely, cutting out just one beef meal per week would save 40,000 gallons of water per year, or twice as much as would fill a typical home swimming pool.[31]

India, with one in eight of all new consumers, could face major water problems within a couple of decades. As much as one-quarter of its grain harvest could eventually be put at risk through groundwater depletion in its main breadbasket areas such as the Punjab and the Ganges Plain.[32] Also facing severe water problems is China, with 28% of all new consumers. As we have seen in chapter I, several sectors of China already suffer acute water shortages, accentuated in part by the surging demand for grain. More than 400 million Chinese live in regions with water scarcity, to go with 280 million in India, for a combined total of at least 680 million people, or more than twice as many as in the United States and Canada combined.[33]

Consider too some impacts of water shortages in a broader context. At least 180 million tonnes of grain, almost one-tenth of the global harvest, are produced by depleting water supplies. Since the average world grain consumption for all purposes (only half or so as direct food) is one-third of a tonne per person per year, this means that half a billion people are essentially fed by grain produced through unsustainable use of water.[34] Asia, featuring two-thirds of all new consumers, supports roughly three-fifths of the world's people but possesses little over one-third of the world's renewable freshwater. Three large new consumer countries, viz China, India and Pakistan, are officially self-sufficient in grain, though they have at least 380 million malnourished people. Because of declining water supplies and growing populations, they are likely to soon join the ranks of grain importers.

Mexico is another country with fast-rising demand for meat and hence grain, importing well over one-third of its grain. It already experiences severe water shortages in several of its main grainlands, which have to compete with urban demands. Mexico City depends on water pumped from 130 kilometers away and up a kilometer-high slope.[35]

In a still wider context, most of the 80 million people added to the world's population each year are in countries that already suffer water shortages. At the same time, global grain demand has been growing steadily. By 2015 there could be nearly 3 billion people—two-fifths of the projected world population—living in countries that find it difficult or impossible to supply enough water to meet all their citizens' needs.[36] More than 260 international rivers are shared by two or more countries, and their watersheds account for two-fifths of the world's freshwater supply and feature two-fifths of the world's people. Of more than 1800 international water-related disputes during the last 50 years, fully one-quarter were outright hostile, with 37 occasions when rival countries resorted to military violence.[37] At least 51 countries within 17 international river basins are at risk of water disputes during the current decade.[38] This, then, is a further repercussion of the new consumers' demand for ever more meat: water wars, anyone?

Fortunately much can be done to make more efficient use of water to irrigate grainlands. Israeli farmers use networks of perforated plastic tubing, installed on or below the soil's surface and delivering 90% of the water directly to plant roots, by contrast with only 50% or so for more conventional flood or furrow irrigation systems.[39] Regrettably drip irrigation accounts for little more than 1% of the world's irrigated lands.

There is still greater scope to make better use of every last drop of water. It lies with the problem of "perverse" subsidies, so called because they are harmful to not only our environments but our economies as well. They are widespread in the water sector, totalling $50 billion per year. Most governments charge only around 20% of the full cost of supplying water to farmers and other consumers, making the water artificially cheap. This covert subsidy sends a message—however unwittingly—that water must be super plentiful, and thus it encourages farmers to slosh it around wastefully.[40] Were the subsidies to be phased out, as is being attempted in China, South Africa, and Mexico, farmers would use water more efficiently; and were all developing countries—these being where water shortages are likely to become most pronounced—to slash their subsidies, this would go far to eliminating two-thirds of their water losses due to wasteful use.[41]

Note too that perverse subsidies foster undue meat consumption. Meat prices are often held down through large subsidies for grain and water.[42] Consumers are also induced to move up the food chain through dietary fads, taught taste, and social status, all of which can be shifted toward healthier diets through fiscal incentives such as a "food conversion efficiency" tax. The least efficient converters of grain, notably beef, could be highly taxed, while more efficient products, notably poultry, could be moderately taxed.[43] The U.S. Congress and the British government have considered junk food taxes.

Also taxable should be some of the more extravagant uses of water. Each January when the authors go to teach at the University of Cape Town, they leave the airport and immediately pass a shantytown with half a million people who must queue for an hour each dawn to collect a couple of buckets of water from a public stand tap. Farther on their way into town the authors travel through prosperous suburbs with a lot of swimming pools. A similar situation applies in Johannesburg, Rio de Janeiro, New Delhi, Jakarta, Manila, and other cities of new-consumer countries. Of course the affluent citizens should have their swimming pools, two to a house if they like, provided they pay the full cost of the water. The South African government, to its great credit, is heading in this direction. But as mentioned above, governments generally charge only a small fraction of the cost. Why does this situation persist, a situation as economically inefficient as it is socially inequitable? The answer seems to lie with civilizations thousands of years ago, often in semiarid regions of the Middle East, where water was both scarce and viewed as so fundamental to life that any charge at all was simply immoral. Today water is much scarcer per person, and "full cost pricing" would cause consumers to ponder their use of it.

The Future Outlook

The new consumers' desire for ever-more meat is set to persist for the foreseeable future. To reiterate a basic point: in developing countries as a whole, demand is projected to grow by more than 90% during 1997–2020 (developed countries only by 16%). This will bring the developing-country demand to two-thirds of worldwide demand, with the new consumer countries in the lead.[44]

Overall, the new consumers' steep increase in meat consumption is to be viewed in terms of its capacity for knock-on effects. It fosters land degradation, it aggravates grain shortages both domestic and international, it worsens water deficits, it promotes global warming, and it harms human health. To reiterate a key point: the 20 new-consumer countries already account for half of the world's consumption of meat, with almost a four-fifths increase during the 1990s and with a still larger increase envisaged for the present decade. This will have profound consequences for the other 2.6 billion people in the 20 countries, as it will for still larger communities farther afield that must compete in the world's grain markets. To cite Lester Brown, president of the Earth Policy Institute in Washington DC: however little Americans may be inclined to heed water deficits in faraway China, they may soon note a difference in bread prices at their checkout counters[45].

To sum it all up, consider the side effects of meat consumption in the world's number one meat eater in per-capita terms, the United States. The annual beef consumption of a typical American family of four requires more than 260 gallons of fuel and releases 2.5 tonnes of CO_2 into the atmosphere (through machinery on farms and through transport from countryside to cities), or as much as an average car over six months.[46] This is a meat consumption pattern pursued by many new consumers who want to enjoy the good life as represented by what they see as the American dream.

The Carnivorous Culture

Finally, let us take a closer look at the health impacts of the carnivorous culture. With its fatty and calorific foods such as grain-fed steaks, hamburgers, and hot dogs, it contributes strongly to the fast-growing pandemic of obesity in developed and developing countries alike. In fact the number of people who are overfed and overweight, 1.1 billion worldwide, far exceeds the number who are underfed and underweight, 840 million. Obesity can be equated with ageing 20 years, and the time may arrive when as many people die from being overfed as from being hungry.[47] In the United States, 6 out of 10 adults are overweight, and 5 out of 10 in Britain and Germany. Nor is the pandemic confined to adults; many children are so afflicted that they may die before their parents. Among the new-consumer countries, Russia features well over 1 in 5 adults overweight, Brazil, Colombia, and Iran 3, and China almost 2, all figures rising fast.[48]

The United States with its "supersize" and "value" meals has become a country of fast fat and junk-food junkies. It features more people on diets than ever before, and more obese people, too. Obesity-related illnesses—ranging from heart disease and strokes to diabetes and cancer, and often brought on in part by gorging on grain-fed meats—cost around $120 billion annually (two and a half times more than smoking-related costs), plus another $33 billion spent on weight-loss schemes and dietary drugs. The combined total is far more than the country's fast-food industry's annual revenues of $110 billion.[49] Every year these obesity-related illnesses kill 300,000 Americans, compared with 400,000 killed by cigarettes, the latter figure being on the decline.[50] In China there are now more than 1000 foreign-based fast-food outlets, and the swiftly spreading fad of fatty meats threatens to bring on an epidemic of heart disease.[51] During the period 2000–2020, China is expected to suffer an increase in heart attacks of 21%, followed by Russia (26%), Indonesia (33%), India (45%), Mexico (95%), and Saudi Arabia (101%), many such attacks being due in part to obesity.[52] In all the 20 new-consumer countries except South Africa, fatty foods could eventually cause as many additional premature deaths as deaths from AIDS. Already 130 million Chinese, the majority of them among the new consumers, have high blood pressure, almost half as many again as in 1990, while every third Chinese has elevated cholesterol levels.[53] In addition, meat consumption in China has become closely linked to recent increases in breast cancer and colorectal cancer. All health-care costs from obesity could eventually run into the hundreds of billions of dollars.[54]

Let us take the point further. If each American cut his or her meat consumption by just 5% (roughly the same as eating one less meat dish a week), that would save enough grain to make up the diets of 150 million malnourished people. Yet since 1990 Americans' meat consumption has risen by almost one-tenth. In Europe, by contrast, there has already been a decline of one meat dish a week, consumption being down from 1990 by one-seventh.[55]

As noted, meat consumption extends beyond steaks. The fast-food industry—hamburgers, frankfurters, and the like—is a bedrock of American cuisine. Every day one-quarter of all American adults visits a fast-food outlet. The industry is now spreading its tentacles far and wide toward the new consumers, in fact it has become one of America's most prominent exports.[56] A good part of the McDonald's advertising budget is directed at the vast potential markets of the new consumer countries.[57] Big Food uses lobbying, educational materials, and contracts with schools' food services to influence youngsters' eating habits. Advertising and sales campaigns are quick to equate grain-fed beef with a developing country's prestige. The carnivore culture has many eager customers insofar as climbing the "animal protein ladder" becomes a hallmark of material success. When the first McDonald's opened in Beijing in 1992, thousands of people queued for hours to be among the first customers. To cite an advert, "Enjoy our hamburger and join the Western world." To put a new twist on an old saying, you are what you eat.

CHAPTER IV

Further Resource Linkages: Household Electricity, Eco-Footprints, and Human Numbers

NOW FOR A third sector, household electricity, that reflects the new consumers' spending patterns as they enjoy the "good life." It reflects the many appliances, lighting and cooling/heating systems, and electronic devices such as TVs and computers that are prized by the new consumers. Certainly such products have brought much convenience and pleasure to households in their hundreds of millions. At the same time, the electricity used to power these appliances and devices entails strong environmental repercussions. Together with cars, household electricity is responsible for two-thirds of CO_2 emissions attributable to consumer activities, plus three-fifths of other air pollutants, as well as much water pollution.[1]

This chapter reviews the role of household electricity and considers ways to relieve its environmental impacts. It then goes on to consider an assessment of all consumption impacts taken together in the form of "ecological footprints." It concludes with a look at still another big-picture factor, population growth, and its role in relation to consumption.

Household Electricity

The world's demand for electricity is likely to increase by three-quarters by 2025, 90% of it being derived from fossil fuels with their pollutants, especially CO_2[2]. Most of this growth is expected to occur in just seven leading new consumer countries: China, India, South Korea, Indonesia, Mexico, Brazil, and Russia. Between one-eighth and one-quarter of all new-consumer countries' electricity today is used in households.[3] In turn, the great bulk of household electricity, almost all derived from fossil fuels, is consumed by the new consumers since they are the ones who can afford household appliances such as refrigerators, freezers, air conditioners, washing machines, clothes driers, and microwave ovens, plus televisions, video recorders, and personal computers among other perquisites of affluent lifestyles.[4] As in the case of cars, household appliances are viewed in many countries as status symbols for the newly affluent.

Much the same considerations apply to fossil fuels' pollutants. On a local level the consequences are acid rain and urban smog among several other pollution impacts. At a global level, and much more significantly in the long run, are CO_2 emissions as far and away the main source of global warming processes. While these emissions on the part of new-consumer countries do not remotely match those of the rich countries on either a nationwide or a per-capita basis, they are sizeable and rising fast. In 2001, China accounted for more than 12% of global CO_2 emissions from fossil fuels, making it the second largest emitter though way behind the United States with twice as large a share. Far behind again in third place was Russia with 7%, followed by India in fifth place with 4%.[5] Just these three new-consumer countries thus accounted for 23% of global emissions, slightly less than the United States even though they possessed 40% of the world's population by contrast with the United States' 4.6%. Details as of 2001 for all 20 new-consumer countries are set out in table IV.1.

Still more significant were per-capita emissions of CO_2. The leader of the new-consumer countries in 2001 was oil-rich Saudi Arabia with

14.7 tonnes, second was Russia, also oil rich, with 11.2 tonnes, third was South Korea with 9.4 tonnes, and fourth was South Africa with 8.7 tonnes. China and India, the two "biggie" new-consumer countries, recorded 2.4 and 0.9 tonnes respectively, while the lowest was Pakistan with 0.7 tonnes. All these were to be compared with the United States' 20.2 tonnes.

At nationwide level, the greatest increases during 1990–2001 were recorded by Thailand, Indonesia, and Malaysia, whose CO_2 emissions more than doubled. Several other countries recorded large increases, notably South Korea with 89%, China with 35%, and India 62% (see table IV.1). By contrast, the United States came out with only 15%, but its 2001 total, 5.7 billion tonnes of CO_2, was 77% that of these 17 new-consumer countries, even though it had less than 10% of their populations.

TABLE IV.1 **CO_2 Emissions in 2001 from Fossil Fuels**

Country	CO_2 total, million tonnes	% of world	% increase 1990–2001	CO_2 per capita, tonnes
China	3050	12.7	35	2.4
India	922	3.8	62	0.9
South Korea	443	1.8	89	9.4
Philippines	68	0.3	65	0.9
Indonesia	320	1.3	110	1.5
Malaysia	133	0.6	104	5.6
Thailand	178	0.7	111	2.8
Pakistan	107	0.4	59	0.7
Iran	330	1.4	62	5.1
Saudi Arabia	310	1.3	45	14.7
South Africa	386	1.6	30	8.7
Brazil	351	1.5	39	2.1
Argentina	128	0.5	23	3.4
Venezuela	141	0.6	28	5.8
Colombia	55	0.2	33	1.3
Mexico	352	1.5	14	3.5
Turkey	184	0.8	42	2.7
Poland	288	1.2	-12	7.4
Ukraine	354	1.5	-38	7.2
Russia	1614	6.7	-23	11.2
Totals	9714	40.4	—	—
USA	5740	24.0	15	20.2
World	24,084	100.0	11	3.9

Source: Energy Information Administration International Energy Database, 2003 (www.eia.doe.gov/emeu/international.contents.html).

We have noted that between one-eighth and one-quarter of a new-consumer country's electricity is accounted for by household needs, and the great part of that is attributable to the new consumers. Let's look a little more closely; how much, specifically, is that share? In South Korea where the new consumers make up almost the entire population, the answer is plain enough: virtually the whole lot. But what about Thailand where the new consumers make up only one-third of the population, or India with one-eighth: what shall we say there? In Thailand the top earners spend almost three times more on household electricity than the national average, while in India the two top income groups spend five times more than does the rest of the population.[6] So a working estimate can be virtually the whole lot again, on the grounds that only the affluent can afford household appliances, whereas the poor can manage little more than a few light bulbs. Still more to the point, two billion people in developing countries have no electricity at all. All the more, then, we can reasonably assume that the new consumers use the great bulk of household electricity.

During the period 1989–1999, China's household consumption of electricity grew at an annual average rate of 14%, more than tripling in just 10 years, largely because of soaring sales of household appliances.[7] In South Korea the annual rate of increase was 11%, in Indonesia it was 13%, in Thailand 25%, and in Philippines 28%. Overall, household appliances are the fastest growing energy users after cars.[8]

Fortunately there are many ways for the new consumers—and the "old" consumers as well—to restrict their electricity consumption.[9] First is simply to switch off wasteful consumption. Consider, for instance, those devices left in standby mode, notably TVs, videos, and other machines that draw power 24 hours a day while switched off but not unplugged. These devices can consume more electricity while "asleep" than when playing or recording. Many microwave ovens consume more electricity by powering the clock and keypad in standby than by cooking food. In American households, standby consumes electricity worth at least $3.5 billion a year.[10] All in all, as much as one-fifth of appliance electricity can be lost while in standby mode, even though this "leaking" can be reduced by three-quarters by equipping appliances with remote-control, network-sensing, and digital-display features.[11]

Still more to the point is to simply turn off appliances that are left switched on without serving any purpose at all. Note a success story in Bangkok. At 9:00 p.m. on a given weekday evening, all major television stations show a big dial with the city's current use of electricity. Once the dial appears on the screen, every viewer is asked to go and turn off unnecessary lights and appliances (not just those in standby). As viewers watch, electricity often drops by enough to shut down two moderate-size coal-fired power plants. This also reminds viewers that the individual can make a stark difference. And of course energy saving makes both sense and money.

There are many other forms of energy efficiency, with latest technologies offering energy savings as high as 75% or more.[12] Consider the positive experiences of the United States, its energy-guzzling tendencies notwithstanding. Household appliances now use two-thirds less power than formerly. President Clinton introduced new efficiency standards through his Energy Star program for appliances such as refrigerators and washing machines, also light bulbs. Unfortunately President Bush has been relaxing these standards, despite the fact that if just one in five of American consumers were to purchase one of the most efficient refrigerators available, the electricity savings would eliminate the need for four large coal-fired power plants (the appliance would also offer the purchaser an eventual saving of at least $500, possibly twice as much, during the appliance's average 15-year life). Similarly, the best new U.S. air conditioners would save enough energy to avoid the construction of 120 power plants by 2010. The Department of Energy's washing machine standards will, over the next three decades, save electricity equal to five coal-fired power plants—and that will reduce air pollution equal to that produced by four million cars, and save 11 trillion gallons of water.[13] Overall, additional efficiency gains of up to 30% are possible by targeting the least life-cycle cost for appliances. This would also enable developed countries to eliminate greenhouse gas emissions by 2010 equivalent to removing more than 100 million cars from their roads.[14]

There are parallel success stories in Western Europe. The best washing machines use 50% less energy, plus 40% less water, and can easily be recycled. Dishwashers sporting an Eco-label use 30–40% less energy and refrigerators 60% less.[15] Consider too the electronic scope for an "intelligent house" where most electricity components, from the heating system to the refrigerator, can communicate with each other and with the outside world. According to the American energy expert Jeff Romm, such a setup can optimize energy use and thus help the inhabitants to live in a more sustainable fashion.[16] The house can feature a heating system that is connected to the weather forecasting system for optimum heating, and that, jointly with other electrical appliances within the house, can communicate with the power company to lower energy demand when energy prices are high. Refrigerators can be programmed not only to keep track of what food they contain, but to recommend a menu based on seasonal organic food grown locally, thus reducing CO_2 emissions.

On top of energy efficiency, there is vast scope for clean and renewable sources of energy. Wind power has multiplied fourfold during a recent six-year period,[17] a growth rate matched only by the computer industry. Denmark now gets 21% of its electricity from wind. This innovative form of energy costs 3–4 cents per kilowatt hour, much the same as coal—though when indirect health and environmental costs are factored in, coal's price is more like 5 or even 8 cents (coal dust alone has cost U.S. taxpayers $35 billion in monetary and medical benefits to former miners since 1973). All current U.S. electricity needs could be met with wind in just three unusually breezy states: North Dakota, Kansas, and Texas. In fact, the United States' potential makes it the Saudi Arabia of wind power, closely followed by two new-consumer countries, India and Brazil. Moreover there is big money in wind. In Iowa a wind turbine occupying just one-tenth of a hectare can easily earn a farmer $2000 in royalties per year while providing the local community with $100,000 of electricity. A more usual crop, corn, would generate $100, tops.[18]

Another alternative to fossil fuel is solar energy. Consumer products such as solar calculators and watches are now commonplace, and increasingly in use are photovoltaic-cell-powered signs and emergency telephones on freeways, also parking meters and remote telecommunications. More than one million homes now get their electricity from solar cells. In 2001 world solar cell production soared by 36%, by contrast with fossil-fuel consumption that in 2001 declined by 1.1%. Solar cells now cost as little as $3.50 per watt, sometimes a mere $2, and hence are as cheap as fossil fuels and often cheaper.[19] Were the latest PV technology to be installed on all suitable roofs in Britain, a country notorious for its cloudy skies, it would generate more electricity than the country now consumes each year.[20]

Finally, note the profits to be made from clean and renewables. The market is expected to grow from $7 billion in 2000 to $82 billion in 2010.[21]

So there is much helpful experience for the new consumers to draw on, enabling them to leapfrog many of the outdated and inefficient electricity technologies. Fortunately certain new-consumer countries, notably China and India, have made strenuous efforts to "decarbonize" their economic development. China has even reduced its CO_2/GNI trend at a rate far better than that of the United States.[22] China has long promoted a shift toward clean and renewable energy while also reducing energy consumption overall. Its Energy Conservation Law of 1997 should cut the country's energy consumption by more than one-third by 2020. Just improved standards for washing machines, televisions, and fluorescent light bulbs could obviate the need for ten large coal-fired power plants by 2010.[23] Similarly, Thailand's energy-efficiency labeling scheme has helped increase the market share of single-door refrigerators from 12% in 1996 to 96% just two years later.[24]

Note in particular the potential for fluorescent light bulbs. China is the world's leading producer of this prime energy-saving device. Lighting a house with conventional incandescent bulbs can account for an extravagant one-fifth of all household electricity. A compact fluorescent bulb uses only one-quarter as much as an incandescent, it lasts 10 times longer, and over the course of its life it can save up to 12 times its cost. In fact it is generally cheaper for a country to give away such bulbs than to run fossil-fuel power plants to energize incandescent bulbs.[25] Over its lifetime one such bulb will avoid putting into the atmosphere a whole tonne of CO_2 from a typical coal-fired power plant. All told, the world's two billion fluorescent bulbs today have eliminated the need for forty medium-size coal-fired power plants.[26] In India replacing traditional incandescent light bulbs with energy-efficient fluorescent bulbs could cut household electricity by almost one-third, and the initial cash outlay could be recovered within less than six months.[27] If each household in the United States were to replace four conventional 100-watt bulbs with fluorescents, that would eliminate the need for 30 power plants with their huge CO_2 emissions.[28]

Ecological Footprints

Having looked at three major resource sectors—cars, meat, and household electricity—let us now consider consumption's impact on all environmental resources and as demonstrated through the concept of "ecological footprints," which measures the impact of a country's consumption on lands outside its own borders. This makes a useful way to assess environmental consequences in terms of the land and water required to produce the resources consumed and to assimilate the wastes generated, all using predominant technologies.[29] The "biologically productive space" in question includes croplands, pastures, forests, water bodies, land for infrastructure (industry, housing, roads, energy plants, etc.), and environments to absorb pollutants and other wastes, especially from fossil fuels. The eco-footprints of virtually all countries have been increasing for several decades, and, in the absence of much stronger environmental safeguards, are likely to continue increasing for the foreseeable future—and at an ever-increasing rate.

The authors' daily lifestyles mean their own footprints extend as far afield as the coffee plantations of Kenya, the orange fields of Morocco, the wheat prairies of Kansas, the copper mines of Chile, the sheep ranches of New Zealand, the tropical forests of Malaysia, among other far-flung places, together with those parts of the Earth's atmosphere that absorb their CO_2 and other emissions. A North American city with a population of 650,000 requires 30,000 square kilometers of land to meet its household needs alone, apart from the much larger environmental demands of industry. By comparison, a similar-size city in India requires less than one-tenth as much. The Netherlands, a country of 40,000 square kilometers, effectively appropriates at least 100,000 square kilometres of overseas agricultural land, mostly in developing countries, just to grow its food.[30] The average footprint worldwide is 2.3 global hectares (GHs), which is a little larger than three football pitches; 1 GH is 1 hectare of biologically productive space with world-average productivity. Yet the amount available to satisfy this consumer demand is only 1.9 GH. Since 1961 humankind (using current technologies) has increased its load on the planet from 70% to 120%, meaning we have already exceeded the planet's carrying capacity by one-fifth.[31] An American's footprint is 9.7 GHs, satisfied by only 5.3 GHs within the United States, meaning the average American has an "ecological deficit" of 4.4 GHs.

In 1999 China recorded an average footprint of 1.5 GHs, but since it had a biological capacity (biocapacity) of only 1.0 GH, it had an ecological deficit of 0.5 GH. The largest of the new-consumer countries' footprints was Russia's, with 4.5 GH and a surplus (because of its huge boreal forests) of 0.4 GHs. The smallest footprints were recorded by Pakistan, India, Indonesia, and Philippines, and all but Indonesia had deficits. Only 8 of the 20 countries had an ecological surplus, all except Argentina being widely forested. For country-by-country details, see table IV.2.

Again, a crucial though accurately unanswerable question arises. If a new-consumer country features an ecological deficit—as is the case for 12 countries—how much of that is due to the new consumers? In the instance of China, a realistic guesstimate is at least 50%, and a similar rough-and-ready approach likely applies to most of the other new-consumer countries. While there is no specific information available, we can gain an initial insight by recalling that the total purchasing power of the new consumers in the 20 countries already approaches that of the United States, that being a country whose footprint is so large that its citizens' lifestyles require almost twice as much biocapacity as is found within its own territory. Or consider the city of London with 7.4 million people, albeit with a per-capita purchasing power of nearly PPP$16,000 per year, by contrast with the average for all new consumer's of around PPP$6000 per year. Every Londoner exerts a

TABLE IV.2 **Ecological Footprints in Global Hectares (GH) Per Person**

Country	Total ecological footprint	Biocapacity	Ecological deficit	Ecological surplus
China	1.54	1.04	0.51	—
India	0.77	0.68	0.09	—
South Korea	3.31	0.73	2.58	—
Philippines	1.17	0.56	0.61	—
Indonesia	1.13	1.82	—	0.69
Malaysia	3.16	3.39	—	0.24
Thailand	1.53	1.37	0.15	—
Pakistan	0.64	0.39	0.25	—
Iran	1.98	0.89	1.08	—
Saudi Arabia	4.07	0.98	3.09	—
South Africa	4.02	2.42	1.60	—
Brazil	2.38	6.03	—	3.65
Argentina	3.03	6.66	—	3.63
Venezuela	2.34	3.28	—	0.95
Colombia	1.34	2.53	—	1.19
Mexico	2.52	1.69	—	0.83
Turkey	1.98	1.23	0.75	—
Poland	3.70	1.63	2.07	—
Ukraine	3.37	1.47	1.90	—
Russia	4.49	4.84	—	0.35
USA	9.70	5.27	4.43	—
World	2.28	1.90	0.38	—

Source: WWF Living Planet Report 2002 (Gland, Switzerland: World Wide Fund for Nature, 2002).

Note: For an explanation of ecological footprints, biocapacity, and deficit/surplus, see text.

footprint of 6.6 GHs, equivalent to eight football fields; the city's total footprint is 475,000 square kilometers, or almost 300 times its geographical area and twice the size of the United Kingdom (or roughly the same as Michigan).[32] London could achieve a one-third reduction of its footprint by 2020, for example by deriving half of its electricity from renewable sources, by recycling all its household paper, cardboard, plastic, glass, ferrous metal, aluminum, and compostables, and by recycling two-thirds of its other materials.[33]

To check on your own footprint, see www.rprogress.org with its 13 measurements.

Population

Now for an issue that is not, strictly speaking, a "resource sector," but is intimately interlinked with the three sectors dealt with earlier. Population is not like the other sectors with their specific economic makeup and their direct environmental impacts. It counts nonetheless, whether in terms of present or future numbers of people.[34] China and India do not have nearly so many new consumers in proportion to their populations as do South Korea, Mexico, or Poland. But purely because of their outsize populations, a proportion of less than one-quarter in China's case still meant 300 million new consumers in 2000, the largest total among all 20 countries, while in India a proportion of one-eighth still meant 130 million new consumers, the second highest total. Both countries' populations are projected during 2003–2010 to expand by 172 million, by contrast with 112 million for the other 18 countries combined. Conversely an average Indian uses only one-seventeenth as much energy as an average American, so whereas India's population is 3.6 times larger than the United States', it uses one-fifth as much energy.[35]

Thus the population picture is not nearly so straightforward as is sometimes suggested. "More people means more problems" speaks much truth but not the whole truth. The myriad relationships between environment and population have been presented in the form of an equation I = PAT, where I stands for impact, P for population, A for affluence, and T for adverse technology. The idea was first devised in 1971,[36] since when it has been frequently refined.[37] All the elements on the right-hand side of the equation interact in complex ways, and not in additive but multiplicative ways, so just one element can exert a powerful linkage with the others.

For instance, most Indians enjoy little affluence, but there are so many of them that their country exerts an exceptionally powerful environmental impact. Conversely, Switzerland has only 7 million people but its per-capita PPP/GNI is the world's second highest at PPP$31,250 (except for Luxembourg with only 400,000 people and PPP$48,100), so it too features a disproportionately huge impact. In many parts of the world, the factor of per-capita growth in consumption is expanding 8–12 times faster than population growth as concerns environmental impacts.[38] At the same time, until at least 2010 sheer population growth will exacerbate CO_2 emissions, especially for countries with per-capita GNI over $10,000.[39] As noted, of particular interest are countries with unusually large multipliers through their outsize populations, such countries including China, India, Indonesia, Pakistan, Brazil, Russia, and Mexico with aggregate populations of almost 3.2 billion (see table IV.3).[40]

The aggregate populations of the 20 countries amounted in 2003 to 3.8 billion, projected to climb by 2010 to almost 4.1 billion, for a 7.5% increase in just 7 years (see table IV.3). While this is far from saying that the new consumers will increase their numbers by the same proportion, it means that in the more affluent countries their numbers will surely rise to some extent by virtue of population growth alone.

As noted, 7 out of the top 10 most populous countries in the world—China, India, Indonesia, Pakistan, Brazil, Russia, and Mexico—are new-consumer countries, and they contain 3.2 billion people, nearly half the world's total. Most of their numbers are still growing. India is adding 18 million people per year, China 8 million, Pakistan 4 million, Indonesia 3.5 million, Mexico 2.5 million, and Brazil 2.3 million. Just these 7 countries, out of 200-plus worldwide, account for almost half of the planet's annual population growth. By contrast, Russia's population is actually declining by around 1 million people per year, and may shrink by 2015 to 133 million; and South Africa's population in 2015 is projected to be one-fifth smaller than it would have been without HIV and AIDS.[41] India will eventually have the largest population in the world, with more than 1.5 billion people in 2050.[42] Already its most populous state, Uttar Pradesh has more than half as many people as the United States. In just the past 10 years, India's population has increased by a size almost equivalent to Brazil's entire population today.

To reiterate the key point, population growth can contribute significantly through consumption to environmental problems.[43] This link-

TABLE IV.3 **Population**

Country	Population 2003, millions	Population growth rate, %	Annual addition, millions	Population 2010, millions
China	1289	0.6	7.7	1366
India	1069	1.7	18.2	1164
South Korea	48	0.7	0.3	50
Philippines	82	2.2	1.8	90
Indonesia	220	1.6	3.5	238
Malaysia	25	2.1	0.5	26
Thailand	63	0.7	0.4	70
Pakistan	149	2.7	4.0	181
Iran	67	1.2	0.8	81
Saudi Arabia	24	2.9	0.7	28
South Africa	44	0.9	0.4	45
Brazil	177	1.3	2.3	191
Argentina	37	1.2	0.4	41
Venezuela	26	1.9	0.5	29
Colombia	44	1.8	0.8	49
Mexico	105	2.4	2.5	113
Turkey	71	1.5	1.1	75
Poland	39	0.0	0.0	38
Ukraine	48	-0.8	-0.4	45
Russia	146	-0.7	-1	137
Totals	3773	—	44.5	4057
USA	292	1.2*	3	309
World	6314	1.3	82	6826

Source: Population Reference Bureau, World Population Data Sheet 2003 (Washington, D.C.: Population Reference Bureau, 2003); United Nations Population Division, *World Population Prospects: The 2000 Revision* (New York: United Nations, 2001).

*Including major immigration.

age is well illustrated by Britain and Bangladesh, though neither is a new-consumer country. Britain has a population growth of just 0.1%, producing only an extra 59,000 people per year to go with today's 59 million. Bangladesh has a growth rate of 2.2%, producing an extra 3.2 million people each year to go with 147 million in 2003. But because each new Briton consumes 45 times more fossil fuels than each new Bangladeshi, Britain's population growth alone causes almost as many CO_2 emissions as the 54 times larger population growth of Bangladesh.

The better news is that a huge amount can still be done to curb population growth, notably by meeting the needs of those many couples, 130 million in developing countries, who want no more children but lack the family planning facilities to put their wish into practice. Their needs should be met on humanitarian grounds anyway, insofar as every couple should be enabled to have as many or as few children as they wish—it is a basic human right. Were their needs to be met, the ultimate global population would be reduced by at least one billion people, and at a funding cost for a developed-world taxpayer equal to a Coke every second month. Overall it should be far easier to change fertility than fossil-fuel consumption.

A further important linkage between new consumers and population is that these people generally have the fewest children (though sometimes more than they want). In India the richest one-fifth have at least one child less than the poorest one-fifth; and much the same applies in many of the other 19 countries. Conversely, the parents of a small family, being relieved of the costs of bringing up many children, have more money to spend on meat, cars, household appliances, and the like. This will apply to new consumers in, notably, Brazil where family size has dropped from 6.1 children in the early 1970s to 2.2 in 2003, and to Iran where it fell from 6.4 to 2.5.[44]

Finally, consider an exceptionally disturbing factor of population in relation to affluence. In India and China, parents reveal a preference for small families even while they still place a high premium on sons rather than daughters. Hence there has been a recent upsurge in both infanticide and feticide of females. The latter method is becoming prominent following the arrival of high-tech machines with the capacity to discern the gender of a fetus toward the end of the first trimester. During the past decade, the number of girls under six in New Delhi, for instance, has slipped from 945 per 1000 boys to 865— and in areas with some of the most affluent neighborhoods, to fewer than 800 girls, these being the areas with best access to abortion facilities. Much the same is happening in China. Professor Amartya Sen, an Indian Nobel Laureate, believes that at least 80 million females have "gone missing" in these two countries during the past few decades.[45]

CHAPTER V

China: A Giant
Awake and Roaring

PARTS OF CHINA have become the new Babylon, and they seem set on becoming the new Manhattan. The country has long had more potential than any other to generate new consumers in large numbers. The middle classes, once denounced as "counter revolutionaries," are now hailed as "advanced productive forces," and they have been playing a hefty role in forging China's headlong economic advance. The country's economy has been achieving far and away the fastest and most enduring growth in the world. During the two decades 1980–2000, economic growth averaged almost 10% per year, enough to double per-capita income every 7 years, thus to surpass South Korea's peak period of 11 years and Japan's 34 years. By 2000 China's GNI reached PPP$5 trillion, making it the world's second largest PPP economy (seventh in conventional dollar terms). Per-capita GNI had risen to almost PPP$4500.[1] This performance enabled one-quarter of a million people to heave themselves out of poverty with every passing week for more than 1000 weeks nonstop.[2]

Its giant economy, led by the new consumers, has made China the world's foremost producer of meat, grain, coal, steel, cement, cotton cloth, textiles, and television sets. The country is the world's number two producer of chemical fertilizers and number three of electricity.

At the same time, it is the world's leading consumer of such basics as grain, meat, coal, steel, and fertilizers.[3]

Much of China's success stems from its being the world's fourth largest industrial power after the United States, Japan, and Germany. It has overtaken Japan to become the leading industrial exporter to the United States. The government has opened up huge sectors of its economy to foreign firms, and Chinese business chiefs are now free to let rip with full entrepreneurial spirit. A further key factor is the low wages, with factory workers often earning a mere one-twentieth as much as in the United States or Japan, and only one-third as much as in Mexico. China now produces 10% of the world's computer monitors, 20% of its refrigerators, 25% of its washing machines, 30% of its air conditioners and TV sets, and 50% of its cameras.[4] Truly it qualifies as factory to the world. Even more to the point, high-tech products, likely to remain in surging demand for the foreseeable future, make up more than one-fifth of all manufactured exports, an increase of two-thirds during just the half decade 1997–2002.[5]

The New Consumers

This is the world's fastest growing consumer society, with exceptionally large numbers of people enjoying incomes far higher than the national average. By 2000 the top one-fifth of the population, 250 million people, enjoyed almost half of national income (and a per-capita consumption of more than PPP$4500).[6] The total of new consumers in 2000 was at least 300 million, meaning that almost one Chinese in four qualified as a new consumer, a large proportion indeed.[7]

The new consumers live mainly in the coastal provinces with their 550 million people, of whom the new consumers make up around half. They are clustered in cities such as Beijing, Shanghai, Tianjin, and Hong Kong.[8] The region comprises only one-seventh of China's land area yet it features two-fifths of the country's population and four-fifths of its economy. It enjoys a per-capita GNI of around PPP$7000, and its better-off citizens enjoy an income nearly six times above urbanites' average countrywide, together with an annual purchasing power of around PPP$30,000.[9] Because the government's economic strategy has long been to "let some get rich first" (farewell to Communism), the new consumers enjoy a host of tax breaks among other supports for private enterprise. Plus incentives for foreign investors. In 2001 alone foreign investors injected more than $40 billion into the eastern seaboard, four-fifths of the nationwide total, further transforming the region.[10] Shanghai in particular is China's homegrown experiment in marketplace forces, with a financial district that is a booming testament to unbridled capitalism. As a result, in 2002 the city's 17 million people enjoyed a per-capita GNI of PPP$22,000.[11]

The coastal provinces constitute the country's center of gravity in not only economic and commercial senses but social and cultural senses too. While Shanghai citizens' food spending is merely one-thirteenth as much as New Yorkers' (the food is much subsidized), they possess 26 computers per 100 households as against 59 in New York, and they enjoy 3.8 doctors per 1000 people, not far behind New York's 4.5 doctors. Here are the bulk of China's televisions, video, and DVD players, cellphones, upmarket cars, and stylish clothes. In the Pudong district of Shanghai there is the new Super Brand Mall, the largest retail venue in developing Asia and with Chinese and Japanese chain stores interspersed with McDonald's and Starbucks.[12] In many respects, affluent Shanghai has more in common with Detroit or Madrid than with cities of inland China.[13]

The new consumers are engaging in a spending splurge for electronic products.[14] China has at least 500 million TVs and 140 million refrigerators, plus similarly sizeable numbers of washing machines, air conditioners, VCRs, and DVDs among other household appliances and electronic devices.[15] Mobile phones have topped 200 million and China has now overtaken Japan and the United States as the world's largest mobile phone market. The 200 million total is growing by 25 million per year.[16] China has also become the third largest personal computer market after the United States and Japan. There are less than 70 million Internet users thus far, but with a predicted annual growth of an exceptional 60%. So too with personal computers, fax machines, and other information-technology equipment: in several recent years the market has ballooned by a whopping 50% annually.[17]

The New Consumers' Future

However startling the present rise and rise of China's new consumers, consider what could lie ahead. Suppose that during the period to 2010 the country's economic growth averages 7% per year, less than the 10% of the past two decades but still twice as much as is considered fine by most governments of the world. This will lead to almost a doubling of the economy and a total approaching PPP$10 trillion by 2010.[18] By 2020 China could well achieve an economy worth PPP$19 trillion, which would make it the world's largest even allowing for solid and sustained growth by the U.S. economy.[19]

This is all the more likely if China's new consumers, both present and prospective, match the business skills of their ethnic counterparts elsewhere. Chinese people outside the homeland are exceptionally enterprising and prosperous. Their diaspora—including not only overseas Chinese in Indonesia, Malaysia, and a good many other countries, but also Taiwan—features 55 million people with a collective GNI in 1999 of more than $1 trillion, roughly the same as for China proper.[20]

There are still other favorable portents. Because of China's one-child population policy, its dependency ratio, reflecting the numbers of workers in relation to the numbers of those too young or old to work, should dip to an exceptionally low level by 2015 or so. Moreover, China is set to make big economic gains from its "worker bulge," having invested substantially in education for both boys and girls. If economic projections hold up, China will by 2030 have more educated people of working age than Europe and North America combined.[21]

At the same time, there is a problem, at least as perceived in some circles, of "unfair" competition from China's low-cost workers outbidding more established countries in the global marketplace. But the world has been here before, with nineteenth century Britain and early twentieth century America, and more recently with the rise of Japan. Trade is never a zero-sum gain: it benefits buyers as well as sellers. If China has an advantage in low-end manufacturing, then other countries could shift to activities that give them a comparative advantage, such as higher-end and value-added goods and services. At least half a billion people in Europe and North America are now benefiting from the low prices and high quality of Chinese goods—and the same phenomenon has enabled one-quarter of a billion Chinese people to escape poverty.

By virtue of the continued economic expansion foreseeable, plus the increasing skewedness of income, the number of new consumers will surely swell at a rate to at least match that of the economy, 7% per year, making for a total in 2010 of more than 600 million.[22]

Meat

The new consumers display a ravenous appetite for meat. Of all meat consumed worldwide, well over one-quarter is by China, mostly on the part of the new consumers. As a carnivore country, this is the world's number one, accounting for well over half of the developing countries' total and four-fifths more than the United States.[23] During just the 1990s, meat consumption per person more than doubled. By 2020 China's meat demand is projected to increase by almost three-fifths, largely on the part of the new consumers.[24]

China's livestock herd is two and a half times larger than the United States'.[25] There is one pig for every three Chinese, making this the pig capital of the world. Pork consumption is five times greater than that of the United States, in second place. By contrast, of the world's cattle only one in ten is in China, less than the United States' one in eight. But beef, though a minor item for new consumers thus far, is projected to double within 13 years.[26] If each Chinese were ever to consume as much beef as today's average American, and if the cattle were to be raised largely on grain, that would require more grain than the entire U.S. grain harvest.[27]

How about mutton and lamb, much of it produced to satisfy the new consumers? Sheep are not raised in feedlots, they graze extensive grasslands in western China. Or rather, they overgraze. The result is devegetation and desertification; and a further result is dust storms extending 1000 kilometers and spreading across to South Korea and Japan, with occasional patches reaching as far as the United States. The land affected by desertification plus the area covered by China's natural deserts already account for one-fifth of the country, with the nearest sand dune only 150 kilometers from Beijing and creeping closer.[28]

As we have seen in chapter III, the new consumers' appetite for meat carries major implications for grain supplies insofar as much meat is raised in feedlots. China is the world's leading producer of both wheat and rice, and the second producer of corn; it grows more than one-fifth of the world's grain on one-fourteenth of the world's croplands. But this may not be enough to satisfy its surging demand for feed grain. A new consumer's diet in China requires three times more grain than the mainly vegetarian diet that is the lot of most Chinese, even though the food energy of a new consumer's diet is only 15% higher.[29] Because of increasing affluence plus population growth, the country's grain demand rises by at least 3 million tonnes a year. During 2000–2002, however, China's grain harvests plunged, with more than 30 million tonnes each year of shortfall between consumption and production (and accounting for a major part of the global grain harvest shortfall). In 2003 the global harvest again fell short of consumption by 93 million tonnes, with China accounting for a record 47 million tonnes.[30]

To produce 1 kilogram of feedlot beef takes 7 kilograms of grain. Because China does not have extensive grazing lands for its cattle like, for example, the United States, the country has to rely on grain for much of its cattle feed, also feed for its huge numbers of pigs and poultry.[31] As a result, the new consumers have markedly increased the pressure on China's grain supplies, and they will continue to do so, only much more so. In fact the burgeoning appetite for meat has accounted for most of the country's recent growth in grain demand, far exceeding that from population growth.[32] By 2000, consumption of grain included one-quarter fed to livestock, though only one-third as much as in the United States.[33]

The time is surely coming when China's meat demand will cause grain demand to markedly exceed production.[34] This implies that a growing amount of grain will have to be imported through international markets that in turn will be under pressure from other major grain importers, notably several other new-consumer countries (see chapter III). By 2010 China may well need to import 40–100 million tonnes of grain (or even more), and by 2020 some 100–200 million tonnes (or even much more).[35] This outcome will affect not only other new-consumer countries, but many other less affluent countries. As China turns to the world grain market, it will drive up grain prices, to the detriment of poor countries that import much of their grain, notably those in the Indian subcontinent and Sub-Saharan Africa. When the Soviet Union suffered a poor harvest in 1972 and had to import grain, the world wheat price surged by one and a half times within just two years.[36]

How likely is it that China could soon become the world's leading importer of grain? Well, there was once doubt that it would ever become the foremost importer of soybeans. In 1994 the government's funding support for grain was diverted away from soybeans, the country's fourth crop after wheat, rice, and corn. As a result, the soybean harvest declined by 2001, even while demand doubled. China went from being a small exporter of soybeans to the world's number one importer, bringing in almost half of its soybean needs in 2001.[37]

If China ever needs to import just one-tenth of its grain supply, it will indeed become the leading grain importer worldwide.[38] Note too that China has a large enough trade surplus with the United States to buy the entire U.S. grain harvest. This means that the 100-plus countries that import U.S. grain would have to compete with the new giant grain consumer. This would create a world food economy dominated by scarcities rather than by surpluses, contrary to the case over most of the last half century. And what if China were eventually to import

20% of its grain, which would be still far less than the 40% or more by Egypt and Iran, let alone the 70% or more imported by Japan and Algeria?[39]

Cars

Because a car is widely viewed as a symbol of wealth and social prestige, in addition to supplying a convenient mode of transportation, China is experiencing one of the highest "motorization" growth rates in the world.[40] The government has declared that the auto sector is to be the chief pillar of the future economy, making cars the primary form of transportation, whereas the main form of travel thus far, the bicycle, is to be hustled into history.[41]

As recently as 1990 there were only 1.6 million cars in China, or less than 1.5 for every 1000 people, but by 2000 the total had risen to 8 million, or 7 for every 1000 people.[42] The government plans that as early as 2010 there will be 17 cars for every 1000 people, equivalent to the situation in Japan in the mid-1960s and South Korea in the mid-1980s. That would mean the cars total would have climbed to around 23 million, nearly three times more than in 2000. This would be an astonishing growth rate, but no more than is demanded by the 300 million new consumers in roughly 75 million households. According to recent surveys, 3 households in 10 plan to buy a car within the foreseeable future.[43] This translates into 90 million cars, or way above today's annual global car output of 40 million. If China maintains the 18% annual average growth in car numbers of the 1990s, its fleet of 8 million in 2000 could increase fivefold as early as 2010. The country would then have 42 million cars (see chapter II). Whatever the plans, China's recent record speaks for itself, with a 2003 jump in car sales of almost three-quarters, making the country the world's fastest-growing car market. During the period 2002–2012 China could well account for around one-fifth of the world's growth in new car sales, or roughly twice as much as in the United States.[44]

If all this comes to pass, China's market for new cars in 2010 should be as large as Japan's today, and by 2020 it could be approaching that of the United States.[45] As a measure of how feasible this is, note that China is already the fourth largest car market in the world, and it aims to become the third largest after the United States and Japan by 2010, with an eventual goal of selling 16 million motor vehicles a year by 2025, when it would have become the largest market of all.[46] Meantime and to help it meet its targets, China has invited in such auto moguls as General Motors, Volkswagen, Citroen, Honda, Toyota, Ford, BMW, Hyundai, and Suzuki.[47] Volkswagen could soon be selling more cars in China than in Germany.

All this brings problems. Beijing now has 16-lane motorways, yet it still features 11 million bicycles, the highest concentration in the world. Result: its roads are among the most accident-prone anywhere.[48] But there are much bigger problems down the road (so to speak). Were China ever to achieve one car for every two people, still less than in the United States today, its fleet would exceed that of the entire world today. And if China's cars were ever to consume fuel at the U.S. gas-guzzling rate, China would need more oil than the world now produces each year.[49] To provide the required roads and parking lots, it would also need to pave at least 150,000 square kilometers of land, most of which would be cropland with an expanse equal to half the country's ricelands. This prognosis is not environmental doomism, rather it has been proposed by the Chinese Academy of Sciences.[50]

Consider too the problem of air pollution from vehicle exhaust, whether particulates, urban smog or acid rain, let alone CO_2 contributions to global warming. China's motor vehicles, of which cars make up more than half, are responsible for at least half of the pollution problem in major cities.[51] Pollution from all sources, including factories, power plants, and the like, has been accounting for almost 300,000 deaths a year in China's cities, where respiratory diseases have become the leading cause of death.[52] The government wants to leapfrog the internal combustion engine by emphasising electric cars, but much of the pollution would then be shifted from the car exhausts to the power stations that use fossil fuels to generate the electricity in the first place.

Until recent cleanup measures, Beijing's air was five times more polluted than that of Los Angeles, and breathing it for a day was equivalent to smoking two packs of unfiltered cigarettes.[53] In view of the upcoming Olympic Games in 2008, the city government is ordering vehicles to convert to liquefied petroleum gas and natural gas, and already many of the capital's buses and taxis run on these less polluting fuels.[54]

Household Electricity

Now consider the electricity used by new consumers for their household appliances and electronic devices. China has become the world's second largest consumer of electricity, with the bulk of household consumption attributable to the new consumers, given that their appliances have been growing by an annual average of one-third (no less!).[55] In the cities, where most new consumers live, more than one-third of homes have air conditioning (a prime user of electricity), twice as many as in 1997.[56] During the 1990s, household electricity consumption grew by an annual average of 14%, meaning a tripling within a decade. During the present decade it is projected to increase at the much slower rate of 5.7% per year (due to market saturation), though still doubling every 12 years. At least 40 million of China's 400 million households have $1000 or more per year to spend on appliances and other "home improvements."[57]

China's economy uses a fearful amount of energy, and consumption per unit of GNI is several times higher than in developed countries. Consumption by the new consumers, while only part of the picture overall, aggravates the problem disproportionately. Fortunately the government has made a solid start on energy efficiency, largely through price reforms. For instance, oil and coal subsidies were slashed in the mid-1990s,[58] whereupon the period 1997–2000 saw China's CO_2 emissions decline by 5% even while its economy grew by 26% (though in 2001 they surged again by 7%).[59] During this same five-year period most other countries were increasing their emissions: Western Europe's by 2%, the United States' by 3% and India's by 9%.[60] Despite China's impressive efficiency measures, however, the country still requires several times as much energy per unit of output as do developed countries. Thus China enjoys great scope to improve its efficiency still further.[61]

China's electricity consumption is projected to grow by half during the present decade, and by a further half during the following decade. Thus far, four-fifths of the country's electricity derives from fossil fuels, especially coal, with all the myriad forms of pollution that entails. Thanks to massive slashing of subsidies, coal burning declined by one-third during just 1996–2000, but in 2001 and 2002 it increased markedly.[62] In 2002 the country's use of coal was more than one-quarter of the global total,[63] and China is the largest emitter of CO_2 after the United States, amounting to 13% of the global total in 2001, though half as much as the United States and with per-capita emissions only one-eighth as much as Americans'.[64] During the period 2000–2020, CO_2 emissions could well double or more, by contrast with industrialized countries' increase of less than one-third.[65] Indeed, China's emissions could eventually approach today's U.S. total.[66]

Fortunately China possesses many alternative sources of energy, notably hydropower, solar energy, and especially wind power.[67] Equally to the point, and as noted, the government is pressing ahead with policy reforms to reduce energy demand as well as supply, notably in households.[68] China has had a Green Lights Program since 1996, promoting energy-efficient lighting technologies. The country will soon start to produce refrigerators that will use only half as much electricity as conventional models[69] (see chapter IV).

Environmental Impacts

China is beset by an array of environmental problems, all reflecting the new consumers' dominance in the national economy. It is not possible to say what proportion of these problems is directly attributable to the new consumers, but plainly it must be sizeable. The biggest such problem lies with air pollution. Despite recent improvements, China's consumption of fossil fuels means that at least 200 million people are exposed to particulate concentrations six times greater than the World Health Organization's limit.[70] Seven of the world's ten most polluted cities are here.[71] On top of this is water pollution. Even though three out of five Chinese cities experience chronic water shortages, four-fifths of industrial and domestic waste is discharged untreated into rivers. Virtually every major river in China is polluted, many of them not even meeting the government's lowest standards.[72] In addition, at least 30% of land in the main population areas is affected by acid rain, which causes over $13 billion of annual damage to the country's forests and farms, plus human health.[73] Some acid rain travels by wind as far as Japan.[74]

To reiterate: a disproportionate share must be due to the new consumers, albeit inadvertently.

Then there is a host of nonpollution problems. Desertification, soil erosion, and suburban sprawl have eliminated more than 350,000 square kilometers of farmland, an expanse as large as France's farmland. Erosion removes possibly more topsoil than in virtually any other country. It is especially harmful in areas of fertile alluvial soils in the coastal provinces, which ironically are also being taken over fastest by urban and industrial expansion. The costs of soil erosion among various other forms of farmland degradation, also deterioration of grasslands, are estimated to total $36 billion per year.[75]

On top of all this are several subsidiary problems. Each year 2000 square kilometers of cropland are paved over through road building, urbanization, and industry growth, albeit only one-fifth as much as in the United States.[76] Consider the amount of land likely to be taken up simply by new factories producing goods for consumers both domestically and internationally. This is related to the problem of internal migrants, being the 120 million workers on the move from rural areas to cities as they seek work. The government plans to eventually employ these people in industry. An average factory employs nearly

100 workers, so employing that many people will require one million new factories, mostly constructed on croplands.[77] The expanded industry will also divert much water away from croplands.

Especially problematical are water shortages. As we have seen, the new consumers are largely responsible for the surging demand for grain-fed meat, and in turn this puts pressure on water supplies. As much as 80% of China's grain comes from irrigated land, by contrast with the United States' 20%. But water supplies are giving out. The North China Plain—roughly China north of the Yangtze River—encompasses two-thirds of the country's croplands, produces two-fifths of its grain, and contains two-fifths of the population, yet it features only one-fifth of the country's surface water.[78] Due to overuse of surface water, the Yellow River in 1997 did not even make it to Shandong Province, the last of the eight provinces it flows through on its way to the sea. Shandong, producing one-fifth of China's corn and one-seventh of its wheat, is more important agriculturally to China than Iowa and Kansas together are to the United States. The Yellow River used to supply half of the province's irrigation water, the rest coming from an aquifer whose water level is falling precipitously. Elsewhere in the Plain and as a result of overpumping of aquifers, the water table fell in the main area by almost 3 meters during just the year 2000, and in some localities by twice as much.[79] The Plain's water deficit already means a loss of grain production that could feed almost all China's malnourished people amounting to every twelfth person.[80]

To counter these water problems, China is engaging in one of the greatest water-moving projects ever known, at huge cost and with great environmental impacts. The government plans to rechannel vast amounts of water from the Yangtze basin to the thirsty north, along three pathways of nearly 1600 kilometers each. The official price tag is $58 billion, making the project twice as expensive as the original estimate for Three Gorges Dam. But since the project will be only half completed by 2010, the Plain's irrigated agriculture could be in deep trouble by then—by which time too China's population is projected to have grown by 77 million more than 2003's total, and competing demands for water by urban and industrial communities will have increased greatly. With water worth easily 70 times as much in industry as in agriculture, farmers almost always lose in competition with cities.[81] Well might China heed the warning of the World Bank that without far greater efficiency of water use, the country is headed for "catastrophic consequences." [82]

Were the time to come when many aquifers no longer supply irrigation water, this would reduce China's grain crop by a sizeable amount. In turn, this would be all the more serious if it occurred at a time when China is finding it ever harder to purchase grain in international markets. Indeed the problem of China's irrigation water and grain deficits has merited an assessment by the U.S. National Intelligence Council on the grounds that it could constitute a threat to food security, and thus to economic and political stability in much of the world.[83]

All in all, China's mammoth size in terms of its economy, of its population and land area too, means that the country's continued economic advance will have an immense impact on environments both national and global.[84] Whereas during the 1990s China's economy grew by 10% per year, environmental damage cost at least 8% of GNI, (possibly twice as much).[85]

Moreover, China's natural-resource prospect is far from propitious. The country supports 21% of the world's population on 7% of the world's arable land and with 6% of the world's freshwater. Although the country is almost exactly the same size as the United States, little more than one-tenth is suitable for major human activities. Most of the western half is desert or mountains, which means that much of the population, along with most of the agriculture and industry, are concentrated into an area roughly equivalent to the United States east of the Mississippi, though with almost five times as many people.[86] China's population, 1.3 billion in 2003, may not reach zero growth before a projected 1.5 billion people in 2025, after which it could decline slightly by 2050.[87] There could be severe problems associated with a population increase of 200 million people (equal to two Mexicos) over the coming quarter century, taking place in a very restricted area, with loss of productive land for urbanization, industry, and transportation networks, and with soaring aspirations for ever-more consumption.[88] In fact, China's huge population and grandiose economic ambitions make it the most important environmental actor in the world except for the United States. Like the United States, China could all but single-handedly precipitate global warming, plus a host of other hazards for all humankind.[89]

The Big Picture

In summary: China is a country with an economy that has posted growth of unparalleled size and speed. Within another two decades it could advance from the world's second largest PPP economy to the first. Despite the fact that around 150 million people are still in poverty, another 300 million are pursuing the consumerist life as fast as they can move. Although they make up less than one-quarter of the population, they command well over half of the country's purchasing power. By 2010 they could easily increase to more than 600 million people, with purchasing power of PPP$3.5 trillion, on a par with half that of the United States' today.

Whether today or in 2010, the impacts will carry profound repercussions at both national and global levels. Consider if:

- each of China's present 1.3 billion people were to consume one extra chicken per year and if that chicken were to be raised primarily on grain, this would account for as much grain as the exports of Canada, one of the world's largest exporters.
- China were to consume seafood at Japan's per-capita rate, it would need 100 million tonnes, more than the world's total catch today.
- the Chinese were to consume wood products at Japan's per-capita rate, their demand would exceed Japan's nine times over.
- China were ever to match the United States for per-capita car

ownership and oil consumption, its cars would emit roughly as much CO_2 as from all the world's transportation today.[90]

Front-rank factor: China's new consumers today amount to 29% of all the 20 countries' new consumers. By 2010 that share could rise to almost 40%. In other words, China is far and away the biggest player in the whole new consumer's arena.

Of course a future scenario could also feature a number of political and socioeconomic problems. Today's China contains a floating population of 120 million workless and landless people who, if they are not enabled to share in the good times, could eventually cause trouble if not turmoil. Then there has been the SARS epidemic, plus a fast-growing outbreak of HIV/AIDS, both of which could markedly cut GNI growth. There is a boom in organized crime and the government is blighted by widespread corruption. All in all, however, China's message is that the Middle Kingdom is finally coming into its own. Suppose that all China's population were one day to achieve a per-capita GNI to match that of South Korea today. Its economy would then total over PPP$22 trillion or more than double that of the United States' today.[91] What if China were then to be spending the same share of its economy as today on military activities, 4%?[92] Recall, for instance, the volatile situation in the Siberia borderlands, where Chinese immigration and Russian emigration have heightened tensions. Could the day come when China's growing military prowess could induce Beijing to take back its "lost territories"?

Bottom line: China is already a giant in the global community and will soon become a dominant giant. Of that there is no doubt. What is in question is what sort of giant will China be, whether in economic, environmental, or political terms. That is a question that we can all ponder, since there could hardly be a more significant factor in our futures.

CHAPTER VI

India: The Second "Biggie"

LONG AN IMPOVERISHED country with poor prospects, India is becoming an economic high flier. The country is no longer "emerging," it is arriving. The country already ranks as the world's eighth industrial power, courtesy of numerous elite business schools, engineering colleges, and science academies, all of which produce some of the world's finest technical minds. For every one student that China sends to university, India sends six. The country's economy has been thriving due to sectors such as information technology, biotechnology, and the media. Revenues from information technology alone jumped from $150 million in 1990 to $4 billion in 1999. By 2008 the sector could account for more than one-third of India's exports, among which software products have been registering annual increases of 50%. Indeed India already features almost one in three of the world's software engineers. In 2001 software exports amounted to one-third of the country's exports and one-seventh of its economy. If China has become the world's factory, India is becoming the world's technology laboratory.[1]

Two decades ago India and China were economic rivals, yet today the average Chinese earns almost twice as much as the typical Indian. With a population only a little more numerous than India's, China's citizens buy one-third more cars and light trucks, 3 times more TV sets, and 12 times more air conditioners. China exports nearly 7 times as much as India does, and enjoys 5% of world trade as against 0.8% (China has recently overtaken Britain as the world's sixth largest trading country). In a single month of 2002, China attracted as much foreign investment as India did in the entire year.[2]

The better news is that India has managed to lift huge numbers of people to an income level where they can enjoy a modicum of affluence. This has been due primarily to India's becoming a card-carrying member of the high-tech club. When we in Britain want to check flight details, we often find an Indian voice on the phone, and it is not a resident of London but of Mumbai (formerly Bombay). Such outsourcing to Indian "call centers" is now practiced by a host of leading developed-world businesses such as Citibank, Prudential Insurance, Standard Chartered, British Telecom, British Airways, and HSBC Bank. According to the management consultancy firm McKinsey, more than 200 of the Fortune 1000 companies now outsource to India, with a market expected to top $60 billion by 2010. They take advantage of India's high-quality and low-cost workers with their sound education and numeracy, and, by contrast with China, their fluency in the English language. As a measure of India's low-cost expertise, note that one of the finest research centers in the world is the M. S. Swaminathan Research Foundation in Chennai (formerly Madras), with its staff of 135 scientists, including 25 with doctorates and 70 with masters of science, working with an annual budget of $400,000, or $3000 per scientist (though worth five times more in PPP terms). Another such institution is the Centre for Science and Environment in New Delhi with 130 staffers and an annual budget of $250,000, paying just $2500 per scientist.

Then there is the associated sector of biotechnology, specially suited to India with its wealth of herbs, germplasm, and microorganisms. The country is home to 16,000 plant species (as many as in all North America), 5000 of them confined to India.[3] Industrialized countries import these bioresources from India in raw form, adding value to them before exporting them as specialized seeds and biomaterials to developing countries, including India itself. India aims to use its own technology to convert such resources into products for world markets. Of the world's herbal-product market of around $60 billion, China enjoys $3 billion, whereas India's share has yet to reach $100 million. Again, this sector potentially means boom times ahead for India's economy.[4]

The scope for future economic success can be further judged by the record of Indians overseas. Whether in the United States, Canada, Britain, Australia, South Africa, or many other countries with sizeable Indian communities, these 20 million emigrants often excel in fields as varied as business, finance, medicine, and law (plus hockey and cricket). There is no doubt about their energy and initiative. What is needed in the homeland is for the entrepreneurial spirit to be further freed from government bureaucracy. Plus, India suffers from cultural and religious traditions that restrict initiative and general stepping out of line. Fortunately the government is taking "break out" measures such as promoting venture capital and deregulating markets. As a result, India, the world's largest political democracy, is on its way to becoming an eminent economic democracy as well.[5]

India's New Consumers

Like China, India already features large numbers of new consumers who have taken advantage of the country's startling economic progress in recent years. Since the early 1990s the economy has grown at an average annual rate as high as 6%, meaning that it has more than doubled. But while India is the second biggest new-consumer country after China, it is a long way behind. Even though its population is four-fifths as large as China's, its PPP economy is less than half as large, while still the world's fourth largest.[6]

How many new consumers are there in India today? A number of economists have probed this question.[7] According to the National Council for Applied Economic Research, the country's prime economic think tank, there could already be 200–250 million middle classers, plus 50 million upper classers.[8] Conversely the National

Treasury points out that only 30 million taxpayers officially qualify for the minimum tax level, albeit huge numbers engage in tax evasion; at the same time, agriculture, being so fundamental to the economy and citizens' well-being, is exempted from tax, meaning that large numbers of affluent farmers do not figure on tax registers. Several experts estimate that in 2000 the new consumers total probably ranged between 100 and 175 million, with a consensus centering on roughly 130 million—an estimate confirming the authors' own calculation.[9] This total is way below China's 300 million, but 1.8 times larger than the third among the 18 other new-consumer countries, Brazil with 75 million.

The new consumers exert a disproportionate influence on economic activities nationwide. As far back as the early 1990s, their consumption of petrol and household appliances—products with major environmental impacts—amounted to 75% of the country's consumption.[10] Today the new consumers account for 85% of private spending on transportation[11] and hence they cause a highly disproportionate amount of CO_2 and other pollutant emissions from fossil fuels.[12]

As a measure of what might well lie ahead, India's economy could continue to post an average annual growth rate of roughly 6% during the present decade, to reach $4.3 trillion by 2010.[13] If so, many of the financial benefits of the growing prosperity will accrue to the 130 million established new consumers, whose numbers will surely have grown by then in line with the economy's expansion. There is also the key factor of skewedness of income, which is likely to become more pronounced during the current decade since it is the top one-fifth of the population who have benefited most from the increased affluence of the past decade.[14] The 2000 total of new consumers could readily soar by an annual rate approaching that of the economy's, to reach a total of 210 million by 2010, or almost one-fifth of the projected population.

India's new consumers already enjoy huge purchasing power. They constitute only one-eighth of the population, but they account for two-fifths of the country's purchasing power.[15] While cars remain a luxury for the elite, the new consumers are keen to expand their purchases to include cellular phones, hi-fi systems, latest-fashion clothing, and other perquisites of what they perceive as the good life. As far back as the mid-1990s consumer goods were increasing at an annual rate of almost 10%, with refrigerators ahead of the average with 13%, color televisions 15%, and washing machines 25%. Three-quarters of middle-class households owned televisions and one-third owned refrigerators and washing machines.[16]

Today consumer spending has maintained momentum and looks as if it could surge still faster. The phenomenon is coinciding with a revolution in communications technology, which intensifies the demonstration effect of foreign goods (even though globalized goods are not displacing local brands as rapidly as elsewhere).[17] There are enough televisions to supply access for half the country's population,[18] which means that even in remote rural villages people are exposed to Western programs with their affluent lifestyles, thus creating "needs" where none were sensed before. There is a long way to go, however, before all the new consumers feel themselves equipped with the "essentials" of their elevated status. Not all middle-class households own a refrigerator, even though temperatures in many parts of the country soar above 32 degrees Celsius. (90 degrees Fahrenheit) for four months of the year.[19]

To reiterate a key point, these many items are sought by the second most numerous consumer market in the developing world. The current total of new consumers equates to two-thirds of American adults. Not that the top 10% in India are anywhere near as consumerist as the bottom 10% in the United States. Part of the reason for the relatively low consumption is that the new consumers are not yet part of a mass-consumption society, still less do they espouse a "throw away" ethos. Most well-to-do Indians do not yet enjoy outsize supermarkets and do not use packaged foods, notably meat, to nearly the same extent as do Americans. Equally to the point, they do not junk refrigerators and cars, or even furniture, within a couple of years after purchase, rather they resell them after many years of use. Nor are India's consumer markets anywhere near as big as China's. For instance, in 2001 India had less than 90 million televisions (83 per 1000 persons), compared to 400 million in China (312), a gap that is not likely to have changed much by today. But India has long been installing as much telephone-switching capacity every year as China.[20]

All this is not to overlook that at least one-quarter of India's people subsist in extreme poverty, and another one-half are a long way from achieving any measure of affluence. Indeed India has well over one-third of the world's poorest people.

Meat

Indians eat little meat due to cultural and religious factors, though they consume large amounts of milk, butter, and other dairy products. An average Indian eats less than 5 kilograms of meat per year, by contrast with China's 50 kilograms and the United States' 122 kilograms—albeit India's new consumers enjoy much more than 5 kilograms. Because there are so many new consumers, the country's total meat consumption is fifth largest of all new-consumer countries, surpassed only by China, Brazil, Mexico, and Russia. Moreover, the new consumers' appetite for meat has been expanding somewhat in recent years, and as incomes continue to rise in the future an ever-larger share of India's population will seek to join the meat eaters.[21]

India possesses less than half as many four-legged livestock animals as China, though it has the largest cattle herd in the world. A few of the livestock are partly fed on grain. Of the increase in worldwide demand for grain and the increase in demand for meat by 2020, India is expected to account for 12% of the first and 4% of the second (compare China's 27% and 41%).[22] Nevertheless by 2020 India could mark up a fourfold increase in meat demand over its early 1990s level. If so, the country's use of feed grain could rise to a level more than 12 times that of the early 1990s, while its grain deficit is expected to grow by somewhere between one-seventh and one-quarter.[23] India today is theoretically self-sufficient in grain, though it should obtain more, whether from domestic or international sources, if only to cater to its 230 million malnourished people.[24] Were India to import grain to support its meat appetite, it would have to do so in marketplace competition with other new-consumer countries, notably China, that also need more feed grain to produce more meat.

Consider what the next two decades could hold if India maintains a per-capita income growth of 6% per year. Let us suppose too that the new consumers' demand for meat, notably grain-fed meat, keeps on climbing at an ever-increasing rate; and let us bear in mind that by 2020 the country may well have 240 million more mouths to feed. In this scenario, grain demand could soar to 375 million tonnes (contrast the 2002 production of 213 million tonnes), and India's "grain gap" could climb to 115 million tonnes. These might seem extravagantly high amounts, but in per-capita terms they are no more than China achieved way back in 1993.[25]

To grow more grain will be difficult. After grain production grew by 175% between the early 1960s and 2000,[26] the traditional sources of growth have largely run their course. Further expansion of irrigated croplands will be more costly than to date, and irrigation must increasingly compete with water users in industry and urban households. Nor is there much scope for further spread of other Green Revolution agrotechnologies. In addition, there has been widespread soil erosion and salinization, among a lengthy list of adverse factors.[27]

There are likely to be water shortages ahead, stemming from the surging demand for grain, and especially for feed grain reflecting the new consumers' yen for meat. Due to its extensive irrigation, India uses more water than most other countries in the world. Most of the country is adequately watered as yet, but by 2025 India could join the list of countries where water shortages prove a severe problem.[28] Well before that date, in fact, several "bread basket" areas could find their grain harvests restricted through lack of irrigation water. Already more than 60% of the Ganges's water flow is extracted for irrigation among other purposes,[29] and water table declines could eventually jeopardize as much as one-quarter of the country's grain harvest—

and this in a country adding 18 million people per year.[30] The time could well come when the enhanced grain demand by the new consumers puts a sizeable strain on India's capacity to keep up with food demands from rich and poor alike.

Cars

Even though India's car numbers more than doubled to 4 million during 1990–96 and topped 6 million in 2000,[31] per-capita car numbers are a lot less than in all the 19 other new-consumer countries except China (see chapter II). A mean figure for the 20 countries was 32 cars per 1000 people. India's 2000 car total was fewer than Chicago's, yet enough to contribute much pollution of several sorts. Motor vehicles include a lot of two- and three-wheelers, though cars consume well over half of all transportation energy[32] and cause well over half of air pollution, which has increased eightfold during 1980–1999 or twice as much as for industry.[33] The health costs of air pollution in Delhi alone have been running at somewhere between $100 million and $400 million per year,[34] though there has been a recent improvement (see below).

India's car total is rising fast, with new-car sales climbing by almost 10% per year. If the economy keeps on expanding at the projected rate of 6% per year, one can fairly expect that cars will continue to increase at the 1990s rate of 12% per year on the grounds that the consumer classes will become affluent more than the rest of the population. This prognosis postulates a total of 19 million cars by 2010 (similar to Brazil's total in the mid 1990s) and 59 million by 2020.

Environmental Impacts

Notwithstanding the many benefits of the consumption outburst, it aggravates certain of India's environmental problems. In the mid-1990s these problems were costing fully 10% of GNI.[35] Air pollution in urban areas levied health costs of $1.3 billion a year, poor water supplies imposed other health costs of $5.7 billion, and soil erosion and deforestation entrained costs of $2.5 billion.[36] Today these costs must be a good deal higher:[37] every time India's economy has doubled, air pollution has risen eightfold;[38] of the 10 cities in the world with the highest levels of air pollution, three are in India.[39]

These problems seem set to grow worse. Many cars run off diesel rather than gasoline. Thanks to generous subsidies, the government has kept diesel prices much lower than gasoline prices, yet diesel particulates cause 10 times more health problems (including cell mutation and hence cancers) than leaded gasoline. In turn, leaded gasoline is 10 times more mutagenic than unleaded, yet many if not most cars use leaded gasoline.[40] Meantime, India's finance minister has chosen to tax a clean fuel known as Compressed Natural Gas (CNG), while giving tax concessions to private cars without offering any counterbalancing incentives for cleaner cars or public transportation. A preferable measure would be to impose an emissions-based tax of sufficient size to push car manufacturers to either improve their engines or to use cleaner fuels like CNG.[41] In fact, one-third of New Delhi's vehicles are now running on CNG, which is a welcome advance given that cars were formerly causing 60% of New Delhi's air pollution.[42]

The most significant form of pollution, though scarcely manifest as yet, lies with CO_2 emissions and their contribution to global warming. Many of these emissions come from the growing fleet of cars, but there are additional emissions from the rapid growth of the new consumers' household appliances, which mostly run on fossil-fuel-derived electricity. Household electricity amounts to almost one-fifth of all commercial energy in the country.[43] More than 700 million Indians lack any electricity at all,[44] hence the household electricity sector is largely confined to the new consumers.

All in all, per-capita energy consumption by India's new consumers causes CO_2 emissions 15 times greater than those of poor people.[45] India ranks among the world's highest CO_2 emitters relative to economic activity, yet it is one of the lowest per-capita emitters, with 1 tonne in 2000.[46] India could eventually prove to be one of the world's leading victims of global warming, not only by losing much of its potential grain harvest to the monsoonal vagaries of global warming.[47] At least as important is the further impact of tidal waves and sea level rise that could eventually cause 20 million coastal people to become environmental refugees.[48]

Probably the most significant factor of all is that India's energy demand could increase by at least one-third between 2000 and 2010, and CO_2 emissions by almost as much.[49] Fortunately India has already gone far to slash subsidies for fossil fuels.[50] Were the government to remove all such wasteful subsidies, that would reduce energy consumption by 7% and cut CO_2 emissions by 13%, as well as boosting India's economy overall.[51] Plainly not all India's environmental problems are due to the new consumers, but equally plainly we can assume that the consumers contribute disproportionately, especially in the case of urban air pollution from cars.

The Big Picture

While India is still perceived as one of the poorest countries, it already features 130 million new consumers, one person in eight. Their purchasing power amounts to more than two-fifths of the national total, or PPP$610 billion in 2000. They exert much environmental injury if only through their purchases of meat and cars, albeit on a level far below that of the long-rich countries of the developed world. Were the economy to keep on growing at 6% per year, then by 2010 the new consumers will likely grow to 210 million, making up almost one-fifth of the projected population and with purchasing power of PPP$1.35 trillion, more than twice as much as today and on a par with Germany today.

Let us end with two quotations. The first is by Bill Clinton: "The world cannot afford for India to be a pygmy. You have to be a giant, and the right kind of giant."[52] The second is by Bill Gates: "India is at once on the cusp of economic greatness and an epidemic of tragic proportions."[53] Gates was referring to a problem that the government prefers to overlook, HIV/AIDS. India already has 4 million infected people, possibly twice as many, and without a strong campaign to slow the epidemic it could have 25 million sufferers by 2010, by comparison with 42 million worldwide in 2003.[54] If that dire threat comes to pass, all new-consumer bets, plus bets for all India's other fine prospects, will be off. But if India takes vigorous and timely measures to tackle the disease, many bets will be on. The country could become a giant indeed, and an unusually benign one at that. The sector at which India excels, software, underpins the primary production resource, namely knowledge, in strong contrast with the traditional resources of capital and labor. India could generate a host of knowledge-driven products and services that will not only boost India's economy but will help prevent many developing countries from taking the destructive environmental paths of the long-rich countries.

Chapter VII

The Big Picture
of 20 Countries

Now for an overall assessment of the 20 new-consumer countries taken together. Let us first review the main findings thus far.

- In 2000 the new consumers totalled 945 million in 17 developing countries and 115 million in three transition countries, for a grand total of 1.06 billion. They comprised 29% of the populations of the 20 countries. Their numbers may well reach 1.6 billion as soon as 2010.

- The aggregate purchasing power of the new consumers was PPP$6.3 trillion in 2000, or two-thirds of the nationwide purchasing power of the 20 countries. It almost matched that of the United States. It could total PPP$11.4 trillion by 2010, or almost one-third of the global total.

- The new consumers owned 125 million of the world's 560 million cars in 2000, totals projected to reach at least 245 million and 800 million by 2010, whereupon the new consumers would account for half of the increase.

- The 20 countries consumed more than half of the world's meat and two-thirds of the world's food grain. In turn they consumed an average of one-quarter of their total grain as feed for livestock. In turn again, the grain connection often caused pro-

nounced problems for water supplies in water-short countries. It
also impinged on grain shortages for the 470 million undernourished people in the 20 countries.

- The new consumers accounted for the great bulk of household
  electricity in their countries, the electricity being mostly derived
  from fossil fuels. Their household electricity consumption
  sometimes accounted for as much as one-quarter of all electricity use countrywide—and it has become the fastest growing
  energy use after cars. Contrast household electricity in developing countries, with an average of almost one-third.

- The new-consumer countries accounted for two-fifths of the
  world's CO_2 emissions from fossil fuels, a share that is set to
  increase markedly by 2010. While the new consumers were far
  from causing all the emissions in their countries, they surely
  caused a significant share if only because of their cars and household electricity. While the countries' emissions did not remotely
  match those of the long-rich countries on either a nationwide or
  a per-capita basis, they were sizeable and rising fast. Just China,
  India, and Russia accounted for almost one-quarter of global
  emissions, slightly less than the United States even though they
  possessed 40% of the world's population by contrast with the
  United States' 4.7%.

- Twelve of the twenty countries' ecological footprints showed
  deficits. South Korea and Saudi Arabia each had eco-deficits
  more than four times their biocapacity. Conversely eight countries featured an ecological surplus, primarily due to their large
  tracts of forest in, for example, Amazonia, Borneo, or Siberia.

- The new consumers possessed almost three-fifths of the world's
  televisions and one-third of its personal computers, both being
  strong influences on their consumption patterns and aspirations
  for Western lifestyles.

Details for all 20 countries, including those discussed in the cases
below, have been set out in tables I.1, I.2, II.1, III.1, IV.1, IV. 2, and IV.3.
They demonstrate that there is a consumer boom of unprecedented
proportions underway in these countries, and hence that there is

already a sizeable community of affluent people in countries that are often perceived as largely poor. In itself this reveals a seismic shift in how we view our world as it moves toward becoming one world: there is a fast rising degree of the "North" in the "South." The findings also demonstrate that certain of the current consumption activities of the 1.1 billion new consumers, patterned on those of the long-rich countries, could impose exceptional environmental problems on both the 20 countries and the global community, with heavy economic penalties (widespread pollution and other waste, energy, and water shortages, and overuse of key natural resources).

So much for an overall assessment thus far. We have already looked at the two leading new-consumer countries, China and India, which in 2000 accounted for two-fifths of all new consumers, the first with a purchasing power of PPP$1.3 trillion and the second with PPP$600 billion. Now we shall consider a few other countries that are notable for the size and growth rates of their economies and populations, among other vital characteristics, and examine them within the context of their regions.

Asia

Asia contains eight new-consumer countries apart from China and India, with 640 million people and 242 million new consumers. They do not compare with the two giants since the combined consumption power of their new consumers, $1.4 trillion, was only a little larger than China's $1.3 trillion. But they are certainly second-rank economic powers already and expanding fast.[1] Many of them were hit by the 1997–98 financial crises, but they all made a fairly strong recovery.[2] And they all have major environmental problems. In 2000 the annual economic losses due to just land degradation in just Southern/South Asia amounted to $10 billion.[3]

We have looked at China as a country of East Asia and India as a country of South Asia. Here we shall consider a country of West Asia, Saudi Arabia.

Saudi Arabia

This country is something of a misfit among the new consumers community. It has been exceptionally rich, now no longer so. It has featured an exceptionally large skewedness of income, now more than ever. Its new consumers total may not expand much in the fore-seeable future, indeed it may even decline.

As would be expected, this oil-rich country enjoys a per-capita GNI of around PPP$11,500, lower than in the past but still second highest of the new-consumer countries and surpassed by only South Korea. It can maintain a daily flow of one-tenth of the world's oil, an amount that it could readily increase by one-third. The Saudi Royal Family has its hands on a tap than controls more than half of the world's spare capacity. At the same time, Saudi Arabia is not a nation as normally understood. It is, literally, the Arabia of the Sauds—a feudal estate, owned by a single family with extensive assets. In return for their loyalty, Saudi citizens pay no taxes, they enjoy free social services (not-ably health and education), and they receive heavily subsidized water and electricity.[4] Yet in terms of human development writ large— health, longevity, education, and other forms of general well-being— the country ranks behind even Libya.[5]

Unfortunately the social contract has long had its day. After several decades of petrodollar extravagance and without really trying to de-velop a modern economy, the kingdom has been in economic trouble. During 1992–2002 the economy grew at an average annual rate of less than 2%, though 4% is projected for 2003 and 3% for 2004.[6] The mar-ketplace can now generate only one job for every two men (women remain largely in purdah). Every year 400,000 young men enter the workplace and fail to find a job. Even for people in work, salaries are half what they were during the country's economic heyday, and less than that when adjusted for inflation.[7]

All this makes for a twitchy populace in a country with a decidedly wobbly economy.[8] Half of all citizens are less than 19 years of age, and within 5 years one-fifth of the population will be leaving home with nowhere to go and not much future to look forward to. As the population has kept on growing at an exceptionally high rate of almost 3% per year, the days of huge petrodollar surpluses have vanished, and the country has a foreign debt of $36 billion, or $1500 per citizen. It also has to finance the luxury needs of the 15,000 royal princes and a vast military.[9]

Not surprisingly, it is difficult to calculate its new consumers today. In 2000 they were estimated to total 13 million people or 60% of a population of 21 million, the second highest proportion of the 10 Asian countries. The total could well be declining, and it could even plunge if the country encounters political upheaval. There is no parliament or any other such democratic body, and people's outlooks have long been shaped by intensely narrow and puritanical religious teaching. Until now: on many a side there is a burgeoning demand for reform of a dozen sorts. When the pressures finally reach bursting point, the outcome could be either a moderate and democratic government seeking to restore full-steam-ahead economic growth, or it could be a fundamentalist affair, at least as restrictive as the present regime and thoroughly anti-West. To many observers, the second is far more likely. In fact, to cite an expert analyst, "If an election were held today, Osama Bin Laden would be elected in a landslide."[10] Thus Saudi Arabia could shortly feature more new consumers, or more probably, fewer than today.

In 1990 Saudi Arabia had 1.6 million cars, a total that climbed by 2000 to no more than 2 million, third lowest for the 10 Asian countries. The country's per-capita CO_2 emissions in 2001 amounted to 14.7 tonnes, the highest level of all the 20 countries, though only 1.3% of total global emissions. As for meat consumption, this was third highest of the 10 Asian countries in 2000, with 46 kilograms per person per year (camel cutlets for dinner?). During the two decades 1980–2000 per-capita consumption rose by a trifling 12%, less than one-third of the next lowest, India. In 2000 imports of grain totalled almost four-fifths of all grain consumption.

Saudi Arabia's eco-footprint is 4.07 global hectares (GHs) per person, the second highest of all the 20 countries. Its ecological deficit is -3.09 GHs, the highest and somewhat comparable to the United States' -4.43 GHs.

Africa

The whole of Africa has just one new-consumer country: South Africa. The country is in a class of its own. With only 44 million people, or 6% of Sub-Saharan Africa's population, its economy is two-fifths as large as all the region's other countries put together. Future new-consumer countries could include Nigeria but it has a long way to go.

South Africa

South Africa is anomalous in that it is somewhere between a developing and a developed country. Its per-capita GNI in 2002 was around PPP$10,000, or six times more than the average for Sub-Saharan Africa, even though the country has a lot of poor people. But its economy has not been flourishing, indeed it has fared more poorly than most new-consumer countries. During the 1990s the economy grew by an average of less than 2% per year, though during 2000–2004 it is expected to have averaged more than 3%. Unfortunately its future economic growth is likely to be severely affected by the AIDS disaster (see below).

In addition, the economy is subject to extreme skewedness of income. In 1994 (latest year with data) the top one-fifth received more than two-thirds of national income, the highest of all the 20 countries and joint highest worldwide. As a further measure of skewedness, the average annual income of the top 10% was 46 times higher than that of the bottom 10%.[11]

White people mostly enjoy a lifestyle akin to that of developed countries, and they amount to 11% of the population or 5 million people. This means that South Africa possesses many more people enjoying Western-style affluence than virtually any other new-consumer country of similar size. The economic status of the country's so called Coloureds can also be characterized as middle class, and they amount to 9% or 4 million. Similarly Asians are almost entirely middle class, and they comprise 2.6% or 1 million people. How many of the blacks, 78% of the population or 34 million people, are middle class is hard to say, but an increasing number qualify. If they constitute just one-fifth of the black community, they total 7 million. These four groups of new consumers total 17 million people, 40% of the population, and this is the number postulated for the new consumers within a 2000 population of 44 million.[12]

Whether South Africa can maintain its track toward prosperity is questionable, and for a reason that does not apply fractionally so strongly to the other 19 countries (at least not yet). As a result of AIDS, the population in 2015 could be one-fifth smaller than it would have been without AIDS, meaning many millions will die.[13] The population growth rate is projected to be shrinking by 2005 or shortly thereafter, not growing again until after 2025. At the same time the economy will be hard hit. Other sub-Saharan countries for which AIDS-impact analyses are available are expected to lose as much as 10–15% of their economies by 2010.[14] In this circumstance, the country's new-consumers total will surely decline disproportionately. The economic impact of AIDS will reflect the tendency for the disease's victims to be people who have not reached 50 years of age, who are still productive, and who are well educated and entrepreneurial— precisely the people whom the country and its economy can least afford to lose, and precisely the people who will include many of the new consumers.

In 2000 South Africa possessed 4.1 million cars, up from 3.4 million in 1990. More significantly, there were 95 cars per 1000 people, the ninth highest of the 20 countries, and 241 per 1000 new consumers, sixth highest. If there is one car per household and four people per household, then the new consumers total according to this indirect reckoning would be 16.4 million, in other words close to the direct estimate of 17 million. CO_2 emissions—perhaps only one-fifth from cars—amounted to 1.6% of the global total in 2001, though per capita they were 8.7 tonnes, fourth highest among the 20 countries.

As for meat consumption, the year 2000 saw South Africans eating a per-capita average of 39 kilograms. Unlike most other new-consumer countries with their increases, the amount reflected a decline from 1990's 41 kilograms. The country is a very slight importer of grain.

South Africa's eco-footprint is 4.0 GHs per person, for a deficit of 1.6 GHs. This means that South Africa is environmentally overstretched, largely through water shortages.

Latin America

Latin America is the opposite of developing Asia in many ways. It possesses 500 million people, by contrast with developing Asia's 3.6 billion. It also enjoys much more development for the most part, with a 2002 per-capita GNI of PPP$7200, by contrast with Asia's PPP$3600 (excluding Japan with its PPP$26,100). Not surprisingly, the region contains only 210 million new consumers, less than one-third of Asia's 670 million, but a much higher proportion of the population, 43% by contrast with 23%. The new-consumer countries in question—Brazil, Argentina, Colombia, Venezuela, and Mexico—contain 78% of the region's population. Their economies show much uneven progress. During the late 1990s recession, Argentina, Colombia, and Venezuela suffered economic declines for at least one year and Brazil's growth slowed markedly. But they all appear to have made moderate or sound recoveries, except Venezuela, whose economy is expected to show irregular recovery for a year or two, and Argentina, which has a long way to go. Mexico has been intermittently troubled, with economic growth of only 0.9% in 2002 but 2.3% in 2003 and a projected 3.7% for 2004.[15]

Brazil

Brazil with its 177 million people is the giant of Latin America. It accounts for more than one-third of the region's population, of its collective GNIs, and of its energy consumption. Of the 500 largest corporations in Latin America, 300 are Brazilian. It ranks ninth among the world's leading PPP economies, ahead of Spain. It has a substantial industrial base, a powerful entrepreneurial class, and a noisy mass media. It is the world's ninth biggest manufacturer of motor vehicles, the eighth biggest of chemical products and instant foods, the seventh biggest of refrigerators and clothing, the sixth biggest of cigarettes and CDs, the fifth biggest of radios, and the fourth biggest beer brewer.[16] The government aims for the country to develop almost as fast over the next 30 years as the United States did during the whole of the nineteenth century. If it manages an annual average growth rate for 2000–2010 of 3.5%, surely feasible, the economy would reach almost PPP$1.7 trillion, or more than Britain's today.

While the country's per-capita income is a prosperous PPP$7250, it features one of the world's greatest skewedness of income and purchasing power. The top one-fifth of the population earns two-thirds of GNI while the bottom two-fifths earn one-thirteenth.[17] It is the world's second largest market for corporate jets, yet at least one-tenth of its citizens are malnourished. Ally a large and vibrant economy to an exceptional skewedness of income and we find that in 2000 Brazil possessed 75 million new consumers, the third highest total of the 20 countries.

Sao Paulo, the center of Brazil's wealth, is easily the biggest industrial agglomeration south of the equator, ranking alongside California's Silicon Valley, the Ruhr region in Germany, and Greater Tokyo.[18] It is also one of the most polluted cities in South America, 90% of the urban smog stemming from motor vehicle emissions. In late 1999 the Sao Paulo government required motorists to leave their cars at home one day a week, a measure that reduced the cars total by 600,000 a day until drivers found ways to dodge it. Contrast the city of Curitiba in southern Brazil that shows the problem of excessive "car culture" can be contained if not curtailed. Although Curitiba's population has doubled since 1974, road traffic has decreased by one-third (see details in chapter II).

As a measure of growing affluence, Brazil's 2 million cars in 1970 increased to 23 million in 2000, the highest new-consumer total and almost doubling during the 1990s. There are 137 cars per 1000 people, sixth highest among the 20 countries; and 314 cars per 1000 new consumers, third highest. Brazil's CO_2 emissions, roughly one-quarter from cars, rank the country sixteenth among the top 20 emitters worldwide in 2001, though in per-capita terms they are little more than one-tenth of the U.S. level.[19]

Brazil is renowned for its meat appetite. Per-capita consumption in 2000 was 77 kilograms, the second highest of the 20 countries and largely attributable to its new consumers. The country has 17 million undernourished people, yet livestock feed grain accounted for well over half of all grain consumption, and Brazil's grain imports were one-fifth of all consumption.[20]

Brazil's eco-footprint is 2.4 GHs per person, with a positive balance of 3.7 GHs, the highest new-consumer country in Latin America. The latter is largely due to the huge carbon sinks in Brazil's Amazonia forest, two-fifths of all tropical forests.

Mexico

Mexico is the only one of the five Latin American new-consumer countries to lie outside South America. Indeed it is a member of the North American Free Trade Organization, also of the Organization for Economic Cooperation and Development (the rich-nations club). But its per-capita GNI in 2002 was only $8540, or one-quarter as much as the United States'. The economy had a rocky record in the mid-1990s, reflected in the 1990s' annual average growth of 2.7%, the fourth lowest of the 17 developing countries. It rebounded to 6.6% in 2000, with an anticipated annual average during 2003–2010 of 4%.[21]

In 2000 the top one-fifth of the population accounted for 57% of national income, the fourth highest of all 20 countries. Mexico then featured 68 million new consumers, 69% of the population. They accounted for 93% of the population's purchasing power, fourth highest of the 20 countries.

Mexico featured more than 10 million cars in 2000, up from fewer than 7 million in 1990. There were 107 cars per 1000 people, and 154 per 1000 new consumers. One-quarter of the country's fleet is located in Mexico City, where they are primarily responsible for the notorious smog and other air pollution. The problem has become so acute that during the 1990s the government invested more than $5 billion on cleanup, but ozone levels remain high, as do particulate concentrations. As yet, CO_2 emissions per capita amount to less than one-sixth those of the United States.

Mexicans eat a lot of meat. The 2000 amount of 56 kilograms per person was fourth highest of the 20 countries, though less than half as much as the United States. Grain imports in 2000 were 36% of grain consumption. Five million Mexicans are undernourished.

There is a further aspect to Mexico's "meat culture," one that applies to several other new-consumer countries: water shortages, which are aggravated in certain areas by the need to grow feed grain. One Mexican in eight has no ready access to drinking water, while many others pay dearly for water trucked in. At the same time, almost three-quarters of the country's water, whether on the surface or underground, is so contaminated that it is a danger to public health. The country needs to spend at least $30 billion over the next decade to enable water supplies to keep pace with the population's growing needs. In particular, Mexico City, home to nearly 20 million people, is lowering its huge underground aquifer by as much as 3.5 meters per year. Now that the aquifer is at risk of running dry, the city pumps water 1.2 kilometers uphill and from as much as 130 kilometers away.[22] Worse, half of that supply trickles away in leaks.[23] Mexico City is often viewed as a paradigm of urban disaster and as the archetype of growing environmental problems of many developing-world cities.[24]

Mexico's eco-footprint is 2.52 GHs and its biocapacity is 1.69 GHs, for a surplus 0.83 GHs. All the four Latin American countries enjoy a surplus, Mexico's being the smallest.

Eastern Europe

In this region there are three "transition" countries rather than developing countries. That is, they are industrialized countries that are trying to establish modern market economies. Of the 20-plus countries that made up the former Soviet Union and the Eastern Europe bloc, only three qualify as new-consumer countries: Russia, Poland, and Ukraine. All the rest are too small in terms of population or too poor in terms of economies.

From the mid-1980s until the late 1990s, both Russia and Ukraine experienced severe economic setbacks.[25] Tens of millions of people saw their living standards plunge, largely as a result of the shocks of moving toward market economies. Since 2000, however, both have registered strong economic gains. As for Poland, it averaged a fine annual GNI growth during the 1990s of nearly 5%.[26]

Russia

Russia is the clear leader of the three transition countries, with half as many people again as the other two combined and with an economy more than twice as large as the other two's combined. Not surprisingly, its new consumers number half as many again as the other two. In fact it features the fourth highest total, equal with Mexico, of new consumers among all the 20 countries.

Prior to the collapse of the Soviet Union, Russia's government had been trying for generations to get rid of the middle class. How different today when the middle class is flourishing, though a middle class of a different sort from almost all the other new-consumer countries. It is difficult, for instance, to figure out the numbers of affluent people in a country where government statistics notoriously misreport the economy and where underground activities account for at least two-fifths of the economy. As one analyst has put it, "The Russian middle class is a black box." [27]

Following the Soviet Union's demise, Russia's economy has been a roller-coaster affair. For many years it showed several characteristics of a "failed state." It experienced its worst peacetime industrial depression in a century, with businesses only half as productive as under the Soviet regime. The economy suffered a whopping decline in 1992–94, making it the second-worst-performing industrial economy worldwide (last was Ukraine). As a result, there was near-impoverishment for most people, soaring death rates as a result of breakdowns in the health system, and more new orphans than during World War II.[28]

The years 1995–97 saw the emergent middle class lead the country's charge into the free market.[29] Then in 1998 came another economic crisis, one that all but wiped out the new affluence. The government seemed quite unable to cope. Corruption spread on every side. The most powerful branch of the economy seemed to be organized crime, and the government's budget slumped to half the size of Texas's.[30] Capital flight soared to $150 billion, possibly twice as much, while foreign debt reached $1100 per citizen.[31]

Almost as quickly things picked up once again, and this time in spectacular style. Boosted by soaring oil prices and a devalued rouble, the economy grew by a whopping 9% in 2000, then averaged 4.4% for the next three years.[32] Russia's economy today is one of the fastest growing anywhere, with an average per-capita income in 2002 of almost PPP$8000 (more in the big cities), plus extra income for many from the underground economy.[33] There is vast scope for still further boom growth. The oil fields now rival those of Saudi Arabia, and Russia has become the biggest oil-producing country in the world with the second largest oil exports after Saudi Arabia. In addition, there is a large pool of educated though poorly paid people who are bent on joining the middle class. Yet Russia attracts less foreign investment than the tiny Czech Republic, hence it is hard for the country to develop a broad-based and vibrant economy. Even under a best-case scenario of 5% annual economic growth, Russia by 2015 would achieve a PPP economy less than one-fifth that of the United States today.

Then there is the factor of income skewedness. In the late 1990s, and hence before the latest economic boom, the wealthiest one-tenth of Russians earned nearly two-fifths of national income.[34] There is a further form of income skewedness, this time a geographic one. Virtually all affluent Russians are in the western sector, centered in Moscow, St. Petersburg, and other major cities, while most rural dwellers and citizens in Asian Russia still suffer grinding poverty.[35]

But problems prosper too. Of at least 20 million Russians who were required to file income tax declarations in 2000, fewer than 4 million did so. The government derives only about 15% of its revenues from income taxes, a far smaller proportion than in most Western countries. On top of all this, a layer of super-rich Russians illicitly export at least $20 billion each year. "Russia is one of the most corrupt and criminalized countries."[36]

Given these unusual factors, it is difficult to pin down the number of new consumers because of highly divergent estimates. They could total anywhere from 30% of the population or 44 million people,[37] to 35% or 51 million people,[38] or 45% or 66 million people.[39] The most recent and reliable estimates propose that the middle and upper classes in 2000 accounted for at least 47% of the population, for a total of 68 million people who were mostly spending far in excess of declared earnings on items such as household appliances, personal computers, smart clothing, fancy restaurants, vacations, and cars.[40]

Some 90% of Russia's population, more than 130 million people, live in European Russia, and it is within this community that we find the majority of the new consumers. They are concentrated in the metropolises of Moscow and St. Petersburg, also sprinkled in provincial cities on the Volga River, in the Ural Mountains, and as far east as Vladivostok. They can afford to run a foreign car as opposed to a more breakdown-prone Russian model. They can escape to a weekend dacha that, unlike the makeshift shacks of poorer people, has indoor plumbing and heating. They can afford private medical care. All goes to imbue these "we've arrived" people with a sense of empower-ment,[41] and this latter factor tends to make the new consumers keen to climb still higher on the affluence ladder.

Despite many positive portents, the future is overshadowed by the fact that since the Soviet Union's end the population has shrunk by 5 million to 143 million.[42] This is an unprecedented decline for an indus-trialized country in peacetime. Life expectancy has dropped by three years during the 1990s, to a level far below Western European levels. The infant mortality rate is no better than Sri Lanka's. The fertility rate is only 1.3 children, down from 1.9 in 1990, causing the annual number of live births to drop from 2.5 million to 1.5 million. By the mid-1990s, 70% of women of child-bearing age had had an abortion, and for every child born two pregnancies were terminated. As a result, the population is projected to plunge by almost 20 million (conceiv-ably twice as much) within the coming two decades.[43]

As for environmental concerns, Russia is "arguably the globe's worst national ecological disaster."[44] As much as one-sixth of the country, an area of almost 1 million square kilometers or equal to Texas and California combined, comprises "ecological crisis zones." During the 1990s agricultural land declined by more than one-quarter as a result of soil erosion, desertification, salinization and other forms of degradation. In 185 cities and towns, air and water pollution is 5–10 times above the maximum permissible. Yet in the year 2000 the State Committee of Environmental Protection was abolished, and its func-tions were redirected to the Department of Natural Resources, mean-ing that many of the institutions that pollute the environment are now responsible for the safeguards.[45]

Meantime the most affluent people have been buying cars. In 1990 there were only just over 10 million cars, but the total doubled by 2000. Today's total is not only the second highest of all 20 countries, but it translates into 140 cars per 1000 people, the fourth highest total; and into 300 per 1000 new consumers, again the fourth highest (the top three being Ukraine and Poland, plus Malaysia). All this further argues that there is a sizeable number of people who can afford the supreme perquisite of affluence. But although Russia has almost twice as many people as Germany, its new-car sales in 2000 were only one-quarter as many. Still, as the economy keeps on flourishing, car demand is expected to increase rapidly.

These findings are to be viewed within a context of Russia's overall energy budget. The country is the world's third largest energy consumer after the United States and China, with transportation, mainly cars, accounting for one-fifth of that consumption.[46] Cars, together with other motor vehicles, account for half or more of air pollution in many cities, and more than 90% in Moscow with its three million cars and other private vehicles.[47]

In 2001 Russia's CO_2 emissions amounted to almost 7% of the global total, the highest of the 20 countries except for China with 13%, and the third highest in the world. Per-capita emissions were almost five times more than China's and over half those of the United States. Total emissions declined during 1992–97 by almost one-third, the largest decline apart from Ukraine (these two were the only countries of the 20 to show any decline at all), while per-capita emissions declined by one-quarter, virtually equal with Ukraine. These declines were due more to slashing of fossil-fuel subsidies and steep economic decline than to environmental safeguards.[48] Sadly there has been a recent substantial upturn in emissions.

As for meat, Russians enjoy less than the Chinese, only 40 kilograms per person in 2000 as opposed to 61 kilograms in 1992.[49] Nonetheless, meat consumption has increased pressure on the country's grain supplies. Formerly a major exporter of grain, Russia is now a sizeable importer, with its 2000 imports equal to one-eleventh of production. During the economic recessions of the 1990s and due to pervasive mismanagement, the country's already low grain harvest fell by almost half.[50] In recent years the country has been seeking much food aid, including feed grain. In 2000 the average Russian consumed 150 kilograms of food grain and 225 kilograms of feed grain, making it one of six new consumer countries to consume more feed grain than food grain.

Russia's eco-footprint is 4.5 GHs per capita, highest of the 20 countries. It features a surplus of 0.35 GHs, primarily because of its vast Siberian forests.

Five Economic Superpowers

As we have noted, China's new consumers already display a total spending power on a par with Germany's. India's far surpasses Spain's. These two countries, together with three other leading new-consumer countries, Brazil, Mexico, and Russia, accounted for 44% of the world's population in 2000 and for 24% of the global PPP economy. Of course only a limited part of the latter share is attributable to the purchasing power of their 650 million new consumers, but a sizeable share all the same, roughly reckoned to be one-third. Moreover it is the new consumers, being entrepreneurial people, who provide the spearhead spirit driving rapid economic growth for their entire countries.

By 2010 these five countries are projected to have aggregate populations of almost 3 billion people, still 44% of the world's population. If—not such a big "if"—they keep up their remarkable economic progress, they will likely see their one-quarter share of the global PPP economy expand to approaching one-third. Were China to maintain its recent 7% economic growth rate, its GNI could grow from almost PPP$5 trillion in 2000 to PPP$9.7 trillion as early as 2010, and nearly double by 2020 to PPP$19.1 trillion. (The United States' economy, if achieving an anticipated average annual growth rate of around 3.4%, would expand from $9.6 trillion to $13.2 trillion and $18.5 trillion— the latter total being more than half a trillion less than China's.) India's economy, if it maintains the average 6% growth rate of the past 10 years, could surge from PPP$ 2.4 trillion in 2000 to PPP$4.3 trillion in 2010 and to PPP$7.7 trillion in 2020. Somewhat slower growth is expected for Brazil, Mexico, and Russia, although even with modest predicted growth rates of 3.5%, 4%, and 4% respectively, their economies would grow to PPP$1.7 trillion, PPP$1.2 trillion, and PPP$1.5 trillion respectively by 2010. Overall these five countries could see their joint GNI/PPP$ grow from $10.6 trillion (24% of the global economy) in 2000 to $18.4 trillion in 2010 (30%). For details of the five economic powerhouses, see table VII.1.

In short, these five countries would become capable of redrawing the economic map of the world. They have already demonstrated their capacity for fast economic growth despite recent brief financial crashes in two of them. China has repeatedly doubled its national income in far less than a decade, a feat which took Britain 60 years during the Industrial Revolution, the United States 50 years during the 1800s, and Japan 30 years during the mid- to late 1900s. The purchasing power that Europe built up over the nineteenth century could be replicated by the big five in well under half that time.[51] They would thus become political giants of the world order and pace setters into a new and different future.

They could also qualify as some of the prime sources of grandscale environmental impoverishment, hence of economic impoverishment too. They would want to boost their car fleets, their meat diets (thus their consumption of grain and water), and their fossil-fuel-derived household electricity. Just China with its burgeoning preference for meat could generate water shortages and hence grain shortages on a scale to drive it to seek large grain imports from international markets and thus to sharpen price competition with other grain-short countries that could not afford soaring prices. And in terms of its fossil-fuels combustion and its CO_2 emissions, China alone could go far to dislocate global climate, albeit the government has been taking vigorous measures to curb the problem.

The New Consumers: Present and Future

We have seen the following in year 2000 numbers.

The five economic superpowers had new consumers totalling:

- 61% of the 1059 million new consumers;
- 74% of the 20 countries' populations;
- 24% of the global PPP economy; and

- 22% of the world's purchasing power.

All 20 countries:

- had new consumers totalling 1059 million, 29% of their countries populations, with purchasing power of PPP$6.3 trillion, 23% of the world's;
- accounted for 36% of the world's PPP economies;
- accounted for 40% of the world's CO_2 emissions from fossil fuels;
- consumed 52% of the world's meat, plus 65% of the world's food grain and 38% of its feed grain; and
- owned 22% of the world's cars, 59% of its TVs, and 19% of its personal computers.

Now let us consider the "broad outline" prospect for the year 2010. Sure this analytic territory is a trifle iffy in that 2010 is a long way ahead and there can be all manner of basic changes along the way. Moreover it is tough to postulate a future for so many countries, very different as they are. But while it would be unrealistic to offer estimates that are more specific than is warranted by the evidence available, it would be at least as unrealistic to back off from any estimates at all. The latter stance would imply that we can anticipate nothing of significance in the new consumers' future, a reaction that would be unrealistic given the exceptional importance of the new-consumer phenomenon—whether economically or environmentally, and whether at national or international levels. Here goes, then, with some crystal-ball gazing, as informed as it is inspired.

By 2010 the five economic superpowers could well feature new consumers who:

- total 1088 million people, being 37% of their countries' populations;
- total 68% of the 20 countries' 1589 million new consumers; and who
- account for 20% of the world's purchasing power.

Also by 2010 the 20 countries could well feature new consumers who:

- total 1589 million, 39% of their countries populations;

- account for 43% of the world's PPP economies;
- feature 31% of the world's cars; and who
- wield purchasing power of PPP$11,422 billion, 31% of the world's.

For further details, see tables VII.1 and VII.2.

Globalization

A key factor drives much of the phenomenon of the new consumers, viz globalization. It operates through communications, advertising, marketing, trade, investment, and the media. If it has had much to do with the recent arrival of the new consumers, it will surely have still more to do with the future buildup of their numbers.

Globalization is epitomized by the emergence of a single global

TABLE VII.1. **Five Economic Superpowers**

Country	Population 2000, millions	Population 2010, millions	GNI 2000, PPP$ billions	Estimated GNI 2010, PPP$ billions*	Purchasing power 2000, PPP$	Estimated purchasing power 2010, PPP$ billions***	New consumers 2000, millions	Estimated new consumers 2010, millions	Purchasing power of new consumers 2000, PPP$ billions	Estimated purchasing power of new consumers 2010 PPP$ billions
China	1262	1366	4951	9706	2419	4824	303	615	1267	3535
India	1016	1164	2375	4279	1580	2897	132	210	609	1346
Brazil	170	191	1243	1666	734	973	75	88	641	840
Mexico	98	113	861	1180	678	928	68	79	624	867
Russia	146	137	1165	1540	579	942	68	96	436	866
Totals	2692	2971	10,595	18,371	5990	10,564	646	1088	3577	7454
Share of world	44.3%	43.5%	23.8%	30.2%	21.6%	29.0%	—	—	—	20.5%
World	6071	6826	44,459	60,830	27,657	36,438	—	—	—	—
USA	285	309	9601	13,210	6728	9257	—	—	—	—
Share of world	4.7%	4.5%	21.6%	21.7%	24.3%	24.5%	—	—	—	—

Sources: Global Insight, World Overview December 2002 (www.globalinsight.com) *United Nations Population Division, World Population Prospects: The 2000 Revision* (New York: United Nations Population Division, 2001); International Monetary Fund, World Economic Outlook Database April 2003 (www.imf.org/external/pubs/ftp/weo/2003/01/data/index; World Bank World Development Indicators 2003 Database (www.worldbank.org/data/wdi2003/); and authors' calculations.

*Extrapolated from actual 2002 figures, based on assumed average economic growth rates of 7% for China, 6% for India, 3.5% for Brazil, 4% for Mexico and Russia, 3.3% for the world, and 3.4% for the United States.
**Equates to household consumption.
***Based on the year 2000 ratio of GNI to purchasing power.

market and the unprecedented scope of world trade. As a result of the growing use of advanced technologies—notably electronics, plus the Internet and the World Wide Web—economic globalization has entrained a social and cultural homogenization on an equally world-wide scale. As a result, the new consumers constitute a class of people who often have more in common with their counterparts in other countries than with their fellow citizens. They share lifestyles, out-looks, and aspirations. A new consumer in Shanghai probably sees the

TABLE VII.2. **The New Consumers in 2000 and 2010**

Country	GNI 2002, PPP$ billions	Conversion $1/PPP$1, 2002	Purchasing power 2002, as % of GNI	Purchasing power 2002, PPP$ billions	Economic growth projected 2003–2010%	GNI 2010 PPP$ billions	Purchasing power 2010 PPP$ billions	New consumers 2000 (and % of population)	New consumers 2010 (and % of population)	New consumers purchasing power 2000, PPP$ billions	New consumers purchasing power 2010, PPP$ billions
China	5649	4.67	50	2807	7.0	9706	4824	303 (24)	615 (45)	1267 (52)	3535
India	2685	5.35	68	1817	6.0	4279	2897	132 (13)	210 (18)	609 (39)	1346
South Korea	785	1.66	61	476	5.6	1214	736	45 (96)	48.5 (97)	502 (99)	733
Philippines	342	4.20	65	224	4.6	490	320	33 (43)	36 (40)	150 (75)	232
Indonesia	631	4.21	75	470	4.1	870	650	63 (30)	67 (28)	288 (56)	355
Malaysia	201	2.34	49	98	4.2	279	136	12 (53)	15 (57)	79 (84)	118
Thailand	412	3.37	58	240	4.7	595	347	32 (53)	42 (60)	179 (79)	291
Pakistan	280	4.73	77	215	4.1	386	296	17 (12)	22 (12)	62 (31)	94
Iran	416	3.71	43	178	4.0	569	244	27 (42)	49 (60)	136 (71)	204
Saudi Arabia	246	1.36	46	112	3.1	314	143	13 (61)	17 (61)	78 (87)	124
South Africa	431	3.80	60	260	2.4	521	314	17 (40)	22 (49)	202 (83)	276
Brazil	1265	2.54	58	738	3.5	1666	973	75 (44)	88 (46)	641 (83)	840
Argentina	377	2.45	76	288	2.6	463	353	31 (84)	33 (80)	314 (97)	337
Venezuela	127	1.24	73	93	4.1	175	127	13 (56)	15 (50)	87 (86)	105
Colombia	257	3.21	64	164	3.4	336	215	19 (45)	21 (43)	136 (83)	175
Mexico	862	1.45	79	681	4.0	1180	928	68 (69)	79 (70)	624 (93)	867
Turkey	426	2.45	67	285	3.2	548	366	45 (69)	46 (61)	265 (85)	309
Poland	392	2.22	85	334	3.2	504	430	34 (86)	36 (96)	206 (95)	427
Ukraine	228	6.04	67	152	4.8	332	222	12 (23)	32 (70)	44 (45)	188
Russia	1125	3.65	61	687	4.0	1540	942	68 (47)	96 (70)	436 (79)	866
Totals	17,137	3.30	60	10,319	—	25,967	15,463	1059 (29)	1589 (39)	6305 (67)	11,422
USA	10,110	1.00	70	7077	3.4	13,210	9247	—	—	6728	9257
World	46,916	1.49	60	28,103	3.3	60,830	36,438	—	—	27,657	36,438

Sources: Global Insight, World Overview December 2002 (www.globalinsight.com) United Nations Population Division, *World Population Prospects: The 2000 Revision* (New York: United Nations Population Division, 2001); International Monetary Fund, World Economic Outlook Database April 2003 (www.imf.org/external/pubs/ftp/weo/2003/01/data/index; World Bank World Development Indicators 2003 Database (www.worldbank.org/data/wdi2003/); and authors' calculations.

world more through the eyes of a San Fransiscan than those of a rural dweller in Shanghai's hinterland.

Consider the role of television, probably the most potent medium for manufacturers to parade their products before ever-larger segments of the global community. New consumers in Brazil, South Korea, and Turkey have been buying TVs at rates comparable to their rich-world counterparts, in other words some 4–6 sets per 100 individuals per year.[52] China now has an extensive network of television stations and a proliferation of cable and satellite services, resulting in a TV-based 90% market penetration rate in urban households.[53] In the other outsize new-consumer country, India, there were several hundred television stations feeding into 85 million television sets in 2001, with a viewership of more than 500 million people, or almost half of all citizens, even though the country still had only 83 TVs per 1000 persons, compared to 312 in China.[54]

Then there is the proliferation of personal computers with their databases. In 2001 there were 257 PCs per 1000 people in South Korea, 126 in Malaysia, and 63 in Brazil.[55] In addition there were fax machines, photocopiers, scanners, modems, digital photography, and perhaps the most powerful device of all in the long run, e-mail. All are powerful tools in spreading consumerist lifestyles. See table VII.3 for the comparative number TVs and computers in the 20 countries as of 2000.

There are also nontechnology forms of globalization such as trading in capital flows, goods and services, and personal contacts through international travel. Fortunately there is also some measure of environmental globalization, as witness the number of treaties to manage the world's common property resources ranging from biodiversity and the oceans to the atmosphere and the ozone layer.[56]

Consider especially the globalizing role of the Internet with its impact on the new consumers' wired-up activities. During just the three years 1999–2001 the Internet almost doubled in size, and today more than 600 million people use it, linked by a global network of 170 million host computers.[57] Similarly the World Wide Web in 2001 amounted to 10 billion pages (an elevenfold increase since 1998), bringing even the world's most remote regions into its information network. Every tenth global citizen now goes online to gain news, to send e-mail, to buy goods, or to be entertained.[58]

In China in 2002 almost 60 million people were online, six times more than in 1999, while South Korea's total rose from 6 million to 26 million (though contrast the United States with 166 million onliners, more than one-third of the global total).[59] In 1995 there were just 27,000 Internet hosts in Brazil, in 2000 there were 1.2 million; in China 10,600 and 160,000; in South Korea 38,100 and 864,000; and in Ukraine 2400 and 60,000.[60] Even so, only 10% of people in Brazil have access to the Internet, 5.6% in South Africa, 3.4% in Mexico, 3.3% in China, and

TABLE VII.3. **TVs and Computers in 2000 (millions)**

Country	TVs	PCs
China	397	24
India	86	6
South Korea	17	12
Philippines	14	2
Indonesia	32	2
Malaysia	5	3
Thailand	18	2
Pakistan	21	1
Iran	11	5
Saudi Arabia	6	1
South Africa	7	3
Brazil	60	11
Argentina	12	3
Venezuela	5	1
Colombia	12	2
Mexico	29	7
Turkey	21	3
Poland	16	3
Ukraine	23	1
Russia	80	7
Totals	872	99
USA	239	178
World	1488	529

Source: Authors' calculations based on World Bank, World Development Indicators 2003 Database (www.worldbank.org/data/wdi2003/).

less than 0.5% in India. Still, of the most wired countries in 2001 worldwide, China was third, South Korea fifth, and Brazil ninth.[61]

The new-consumer countries are set to cash in on this techno-revolution. In 1999 more than half of Malaysia's exports were high-tech, as were more than one-quarter of Mexico's and Philippines'. While the principal language used today for activities worldwide is English, it could eventually be overtaken by Chinese.[62]

The scope for globalization to push countries into new eras is illustrated by experiences in Russia of this book's first author. In 1982 he visited Moscow and had occasion to use a photocopier. Not seeing one, he asked where he could find one. An official replied, "We do not allow such machines here because they would foster the underground press." Of course there were government photocopiers and they slowly made their way into the hands of the undergrounders, thus opening up a huge window into the doings of the outside world. In 1986 he returned to Moscow; where, he asked, was a fax machine? "We do not want such machines here, they would infect our Communist system with alien ideas." Of course fax machines were being steadily smuggled into Russia, and each one opened up a torrent of outside information. In 1997 he visited Moscow yet again; where could he receive e-mail? "E-mailing is generally forbidden because a free-for-all communication would be deeply disruptive." Gorbachev admitted that electronic telecommunications were a major reason why he felt he had to pursue Glasnost or "openness": there was no way to hold back the information floods streaming in from the global community.

China enjoys economic freedom but not political freedom. The best way to get that genie out of the bottle would be for Chinese people to let rip with the Internet and make the government swallow the consequences. Whatever one may think about globalization, and there are a lot of eloquent protesters,[63] it has done much to generate the arrival of the new consumers and it seems set to continue along that track, more powerfully year by year.

HIV/AIDS and Other Diseases

Yet another globalized phenomenon throws a shadow over a few countries' prospect for generating many more new consumers in the future: HIV/AIDS. South Africa is not the only new-consumer country to be afflicted. Several other countries could soon be severely stricken too. In China an official estimate in 2001 proposed that only 1 million people were infected with HIV, but the SARS episode showed that government estimates are sometimes inclined to be hugely optimistic, if not downright unrealistic. The true total could have been as many as several million—and China's case load is expanding by 30% per year and hence doubling every 2.3 years, meaning that the 2010 total could easily be as many as 20 million if not more.[64] By comparison, the United States has 900,000 people living with HIV/AIDS, with 40,000 new cases reported every year. Of course 20 million HIV cases in China would be only 2% of around 1 billion people aged 15–65, by contrast with several African countries where at least 20% of the adult population has HIV/AIDS.[65]

India is still worse afflicted, with 4 million people officially infected with HIV/AIDS, out of a total of something over 6.5 million for all of Asia. By 2010 the country could have 20–25 million infections, despite Bill Gates's donation of $100 million to counter the disease. This means of course that China and India together could have at least 40 million cases by 2010, or almost as many as in the entire world in 2002. There are signs of the pandemic also gaining a foothold in Indonesia and Thailand among other Asian countries, and AIDS deaths in Asia are projected to reach 17 million in 2020–2025, by contrast with 28 million worldwide in 2002.[66]

These alarming figures notwithstanding, the epidemic is spreading most quickly of all in Eastern Europe. In Russia the number of reported cases has doubled every year since 1998, due mainly to intravenous drug use. The total is still small, but by 2010 the country could have 7 million sufferers.[67]

All this will eventually mean severe and protracted setbacks for the economies concerned. South Africa, for instance, will lose the equivalent of many years' economic growth.[68] In Russia the economy is predicted to shrink during 2010–2020 by at least 10% as compared with a future without AIDS.[69] In turn, these economic setbacks will reduce the lifestyles of many of today's new consumers, and they will likewise cut back on the emergence of more new consumers in the future.

On top of all this is the threat of other epidemics ahead. At least 30 new diseases have cropped up since the mid-1970s (e.g., the SARS and West Nile viruses, Ebola), causing tens of millions of deaths.[70]

The Have-Nots

There is still another form of globalization at work, being the growing divide between the haves and have-nots. The phenomenon of 1.1 billion new consumers serves to point up the parallel phenomenon of 1.3 billion who not only subsist on incomes of less than $1 per day but who are being left ever further behind. Among the worst off are, for example, the people of Mumbai in India, formerly known as Bombay. Half of the city's 12 million residents are either slum dwellers or homeless. They occupy just one-seventeenth of the city's land, with little or no access to sanitation and sewage facilities. As many as 500 people share one public latrine.

The abject state of those in absolute poverty is accentuated, all too unwittingly of course, by the new affluence in their midst. Neither side presumably recognizes that to some extent at least the poor are poor because the rich are rich, and the new consumers might reflect on their role in, for example, grain and water supplies, these being resources that are not only in shortening supply but should be viewed as so fundamental to human life that they rank as basic human rights for everyone. For the most part, however, trickle-down theory— meaning that rich people generate prosperity for those lower down the income scale—remains theory.

The 1.1 billion new consumers in 2000 enjoyed a collective purchasing power of PPP$6.3 trillion, two-thirds of their national totals. The average was also 16 times more than the cash income of the 1.3 billion people living on less than $1 per day. Even under the most optimistic assumptions, in 2015 the number of people living on less than $2 a day is not likely to fall by more than half a billion from today's 2.8 billion.[71]

Conclusion

The new-consumer countries range across a variety of political systems, degrees of economic advancement, social and cultural contexts, and historical traditions. Yet the new consumers also share much the same aims and aspirations, fostered in major measure by globalization. Hence they constitute a community that often transcends national boundaries. Again: the new consumers are building a new dimension to our world, little recognized though it may be thus far.

CHAPTER VIII

Sustainable Consumption: Where Do We Find It?

WE CAN'T SAY it too often. Consumption has become a dominant phenomenon of our world. It is enjoyed to some degree in virtually all countries and to marked degree by the two billion people—in the long-rich world plus the new consumers—who have enough money to engage in consumption like never before. We are witnessing a consumption boom of a compressed scale beyond the dreams of people in all history. Because it means a leap out of subsistence lifestyles for huge numbers of people, this is something to celebrate to the skies.

Yet it may prove to be a phenomenon with limited shelf life. We cannot indulge in endless overloading of the environmental underpinnings of our economies, whether they be natural resources such as water, vegetation, and other obvious items, or less visible items such as the atmosphere's capacity to absorb CO_2 emissions and other pollutants. Conversely, sustainable consumption—that up-and-coming holy grail—amounts to the maximum that we can consume in a given year without reducing our capacity to consume as much or more next year. In many respects our consumption is consuming the Earth's "productive capacity," especially environmental resources, even though we count that overuse as a bountiful income in our reckonings of GNI. To cite the American economist Paul Hawken, "Our thinking is backwards: we shouldn't use more of what we have less of (natural capital) to use less of what we have more of (people)."[1]

Hence the need to move on toward sustainable consumption forthwith. It should not be so difficult as is often supposed, and it certainly need not be a case of endlessly foregoing this and sacrificing that. On the contrary, it could actually supply us with more fulfilling lifestyles.

The Drivers of Consumption

In order to figure out how to head off in the new direction, we need to look at what impels consumers toward unsustainable consumption. What actually drives the new consumers, especially insofar as their recent arrival may mean they have motivations different from their counterparts in the long-rich countries? Well, there is an obvious reason for hundreds of millions of people: it has not been long since they left behind their penury if not poverty. When once they have achieved affluence, however, what drives them to seek more and more affluence? If they manage to make their wealth grow, will it help the purpose of wealth to grow too? After all, people pursue affluence in order to enjoy the perquisites of an agreeable and secure lifestyle. Would, say, twice as much affluence bring them twice as much of what they truly want?

Let us, then, take a further look at the consumption outburst and ask what underlies this manifestation of affluence. Essentially it reflects what counts for the new consumers: to make money and build a career; look good and stylish; to enjoy a lot of consumerist choices; and to exemplify that well-known credo, "When the going gets tough, the tough go shopping"; and in all these instances to be seen to do so. Okay, virtually all affluent people feel driven to consume, consume, and still more consume. And yet there are emergent signs that consumption does not always enhance people's well-being in the long run. Many consumers, especially in the long-rich world, are finding that the good life does not lie with piling up ever-more goodies. Who on their death beds regrets they had not earned more in order to consume more? As the Chinese say, the person who dies with the most toys still dies.

In fact there are signs that the consumption cult, in its present form at least, may be on the skids.[2] A 2003 global survey shows that when people are asked about reducing consumption, those developed-world citizens in favor total more than 60% of consultees, and in Eastern Europe and Russia 50%, though in developing Asia and Latin America only 30% (still significant). With regard to specific items as viewed by developed-world people, those favoring less consumption of electricity total 83%, of paper 81%, of gasoline and other fuels 73%, of water 71%, and of food 65%. The average for developing countries is, not surprisingly, just 21%. The highest average is Japan's 80%, followed by North America's 67%, Western Europe's 62%, Eastern Europe and Russia's 54%, developing Asia's 31%, and Latin America's 30%.[3]

So what drives many consumers to pursue the Nirvana of ever-greater consumption? Is it a case of "goods are good, so more goods must be better"? True, economic advancement can often equate with human advancement. To the commercial world, however, everything is a product and everyone is a customer, and all values reflect the wisdom of the marketplace. All too often, that equates to the Coke and McDonald's culture, which are far from delivering ultimate well-being.

Nor is there any sense of "enoughness." Why do even the ultrarich people feel compelled to keep racing on the consumption treadmill? Could they sense a motivation that is self-defeating? The stadium metaphor says that if everyone stands up to get a better view, nobody sees any better than if everyone remains seated. Keeping up with the neighbors can become unneighborly. This is what often happens when people focus on conspicuous consumption such as swanky cars and latest-style housing, by contrast with "hidden" consumption such as sports, arts, or even the prosaic-sounding matter of health care.[4] Consumption becomes a case of keeping up with the Joneses at every turn. To cite that noted sociologist Karl Marx, "A house may be large

or small; as long as the surrounding houses are equally small, it satis-
fies all social demands for a dwelling. But let a palace arise beside the
little house, and it shrinks from a little house to a hut."[5] The competition applies equally to our cars, our eating patterns, our electronic
equipment and our vacations.

While forever comparing yourself against others, you can also compare yourself today with yesterday's you. The novelty of a new Mercedes wears off, leaving you yearning for a still bigger and better car.
And what if the Joneses next door have just got themselves a second
Mercedes? It's a kind of endless Red Queen struggle. If you don't possess this or that, you are not a member of the "consumption club." If
you want to belong, you had better go and purchase yet another
membership totem.[6]

The first author of this book was brought up on a small farm in
northern England. The house had no electricity or gas, the family got
water from the same stream as the cattle, and the toilet was a long-
drop affair down the yard. Yet, knowing nothing else and being
located in countryside of surpassing beauty, the family was content
with it. Today that same lifestyle would be considered absurdly "dis-
advantaged."

Nor is there enough "enoughness" in other ways. An American
now enjoys a choice of 50,000 food products, compared with only 100
as many a century ago. Perhaps this is partly what causes many Americans to eat far more than is good for their health. Perhaps too it partly
explains why Americans are so prodigal with their food. More than
one-quarter of food leaving the farm gate is lost by the time it reaches
restaurants and households, whereupon a further one-quarter is
allowed to rot in fridges or is thrown away from overloaded meal
plates.

All this flies in the face of a keystone of our marketplace economies, known to the experts as "consumer sovereignty." It is a concept
viewed as holy writ. It states that the consumer knows best what is
good for him or her, and nobody else knows squits. The concept offers
assertions of this extreme sort even though it implies that the con-

sumer has complete information, which he or she does not, and that spillover costs ("your car pollutes my air") are so trifling that they can be ignored. Moreover consumers' wishes and "wants" are moulded by media images of the good life, whereupon four out of five Americans find they often consume more than they need.[7] Consumers are further influenced by advertising to the tune of $450 billion per year worldwide (as much as half of it in the United States alone, almost $800 per American). The advertising juggernaut is spreading. Developing-world advertising—directed primarily at the new consumers—grew during 1986–96 by 210% in India, 220% in Philippines, 325% in South Korea, 350% in Malaysia and Thailand, 640% in Indonesia, and more than 1000% in China. In terms of advertising spending relative to GNI, the top country in 1996 was Colombia with 2.6% (the United States, 1.3%). During the 1990s advertising expenditures soared 4.1-fold in developing Asia and 5.6-fold in Latin America.[8] "Consumer choice," anyone?

Conversely there is the immense power of a relatively few megacorporations that drive consumption, whether as manufacturers and other producers or as giant retailers and media moguls. Of the world's 100 largest economies, 51 are corporations (not including banking and financial outfits), and only 49 are nation-states. The top 300 corporations own one-quarter of the world's productive assets and of the world's economic output.[9] This financial muscle enables them to exert an exceptionally powerful impact on consumers' outlooks, desires, and shopping patterns. For instance, they persuade consumers to drink bottled water even though that is often no healthier than tap water and can cost one thousand times as much. Those readers who would like to learn about counteradvertising measures could consult *Adbusters,* a magazine with 85,000 circulation, two-thirds of it in the United States (www.adbusters.org).

Fortunately a sizeable supplier of consumerist goods, the fashion industry, is taking steps to promote sustainable consumption. Fashion designers, in conjunction with retail giants ranging from Versace to Marks and Spencer, are reflecting a growing demand for "ethical" and "green" products. A strong supporter is the Web-based global fashion magazine *Lucire,* whose founding publisher Jack Yan says "fashion magazines should not only communicate the labels and their offerings, but they should also give the industry insight into what's hot and what's not."[10] Challenge: how to make fashion sustainable and sustainability fashionable?

Finally, consider an ultimate consequence of these drivers of consumption: affluenza, being "a painful, contagious, socially transmitted condition of overload, debt, anxiety, and waste resulting from the dogged pursuit of endless more."[11] The affluenza epidemic is rooted in the obsessive quest for economic advancement that serves as the American Dream whether in the United States or elsewhere. It has become so widespread that it is now the ultimate goal of virtually all economic, social, and political systems worldwide. It has become a cult classic. Unfortunately its adverse consequences are not so widely hailed. Since 1950 the United States has used up more natural resources than all people who had lived on Earth before then; and in each of the years 1997–2000 more Americans declared bankruptcy than graduated from college.[12]

Fortunately the main forms of treatment of the disease are well known: downshifting to voluntary simplicity; joining in Buy Nothing Days; enjoying more leisure; promoting economic signals of sustainability such as the Genuine Progress Indicator, measuring each individual's ecological footprint; and—probably most important of all—promoting the New American Dream that focuses on quality of life as well as quantity of livelihood.[13] We shall consider several of these affluenza cures in the next chapter.

Eco-Technologies: An Imperative

Now for a different approach to the consumption question: how to help make it sustainable by eliminating our more absurd inefficiencies of raw materials and energy. Consider the "true cost" of a soft-drinks can in Europe. As a result of heavily subsidized transportation (artificially cheap gasoline and diesel for starters) among other driver factors, a can can be much more costly than its drink. Bauxite is mined in Australia before being shipped to Scandinavia where it is smelted into aluminum. It is then shipped to Germany for rolling into aluminum sheets. The material is then shipped again, this time to Britain where it is transformed into cans that are treated and painted. Next, the completed cans are sent to the bottling factory. Eventually the canned drink is packaged and distributed to regional warehouses, and finally to individual stores, before being purchased by the consumer.[14] Were the transportation subsidies and the many other "external" costs to be included in the price, there would be instant efforts to make the whole production process more efficient. An increased price would also persuade consumers to purchase soft drinks when they really want them, rather than when there is nothing much else to do.

We need eco-technologies like crazy—those promoting energy efficiency, recycling, pollution controls, and the lengthy like—in order to counter the grotesque wastefulness of industrial societies. An average of 100 tonnes of nonrenewable materials are effectively consumed, whether directly or indirectly, by each rich-world person every year, or 40 times more than in developing countries. More than 90% of the materials and resources harvested or displaced in nature are wasted on their way to producing food, machines, vehicles, infrastructure, and the like. In the United States, a mere 1% of materials flows ends up in products that are still in use six months after sale, the rest being junked.[15]

Fortunately there is a host of eco-technologies available to cut back on inefficiencies and make us more productive (and again, efficiency fosters sufficiency). In Britain these technologies, especially those that get more work out of, say, each energy unit, mean that one hour's work in a factory produces twice as much as in bygone days. But British workers still feel they need to put in long hours to keep their incomes rising. If they work 47 hours a week for 47 weeks a year for 47 years, they put in 100,000 hours in a lifetime. Today they need only 50,000 hours for the same output because of increased efficiency, but they often persist with many more hours to keep their incomes and consumption on the rise.

As we have seen in several chapters already, there is much we can do to mobilize eco-technologies that foster energy efficiency, better water use, recycling, waste management, pollution controls, closed-loop manufacturing, and zero-emissions industry.[16] In fact there are enough eco-technologies to enable everybody to enjoy twice as much material well-being, while using only half as much raw materials and energy and causing only half as much pollution and other forms of waste. This is known as the Factor Four strategy (twice as much × only half as much), which has been endorsed by a good number of corporations and governments. Even Factor 10 is on its way. This latter is not only an ideal but an imperative, and it illustrates the thesis that there is a growing convergence between the idealist and the realist. The global community needs to cut its use of natural resources by 50% by the year 2050, even while allowing for more people with more demands. Developing countries may lack both the technologies and the inclination to achieve the 50% goal, which means the developed countries that use the great bulk of resources should aim for a 90% cutback.[17]

Thus the rationale for Factor 10. The strategy requires that materials-intensive products be redesigned for repair, reuse, renovation, remanufacturing, and, as a last resort, recycling. Factor Ten is not so way out as it might sound. When the Industrial Revolution enabled workers to substitute coal and machines for human muscle, they expanded worker productivity 100 times within half a century. Bear in mind too that in the last three decades we have slashed energy use in many "best practice" instances by three-quarters. Factor Ten is entering the vocabulary of government officials, economist planners, scientists, and business leaders around the world, and it has been promoted by the World Business Council for Sustainable Development. Several leading corporations such as DuPont, Dow Chemical, Honda, and Panasonic see it as a powerful mode to gain competitive advantage.[18]

Already there is an array of techno-breakthroughs that could help us toward Factor Ten. Consider these: extralight composites stronger than steel; diodes that emit light for 20 years without bulbs; ultrasound washing machines that use no water, heat, or soap; plastics that are both reusable and compostible; roofs and roads that serve as solar-energy collectors; and quantum semiconductors that store vast amounts of information on chips no bigger than a dot. Note too the recycling available for billions of plastic cups thrown away every year, the "waste" being transformed into a host of new stationery products. Worn-out car tires become sandals and mouse pads. Food packaging, carry bags, and refuse holders are being manufactured from 100% degradable polythene. Also remarkable is that London's Heathrow Airport features waterless urinals with biodegradable fluids and recyclable cartridges, replacing conventional urinals that use one-quarter of a million liters of water every year.[19]

It used to take a long time for techno-breakthroughs to reach the public arena. Note the delays before new technologies could reach one-quarter of the U.S. population: electricity 46 years, the telephone 35 years, radio 22 years, television 26 years, and the microwave oven 30 years. Fortunately the process is speeding up. The personal computer has taken only 16 years, the mobile phone 13 years, and the World Wide Web 7 years. But let's believe we can do it, let's beware the naysayers. In 1900 Lord Kelvin, one of Britain's top scientists, declared, "X-rays will prove to be a hoax." In 1922, Thomas Edison believed that "radio has no future." In 1943, Thomas Watson, chairman of IBM, asserted "there is a world market for maybe five computers." In 1956, Richard Wooley, British Astronomer Royal, declared, "Space travel is utter bilge." In 1977, Ken Olson, President of Digital Corporation, stated that "There is no reason anyone would want a computer in their home." In 1981, Bill Gates considered that "640K ought to be enough for anybody."[20]

No doubt about it, we can deploy a host of eco-technologies to help us squeeze through the environmental bottlenecks ahead. In particular, they will enable the developing countries, and especially the new-consumer countries, to avoid the high-throughput, high-pollution, and high-waste route of the so-called developed countries. Instead they can learn how to do far more with far less, and eventually, to cite the efficiency expert Amory Lovins, "to do virtually everything with virtually nothing."[21] Whereas raw materials account for 40% of the value of that icon of the industrial age, the car, they make up 0.3% of the value of that icon of the information-technology age, the microchip—and all the microchips in the world comprise so little volume that they would fit inside a jumbojet. A car amounts to 2 tonnes of materials to get us from here to there, whereas the microchip, by, for example, enabling people to work at home, can often eliminate the need to go from here to there in the first place.

Fortunately there have been some initial efforts in new-consumer countries to foster sustainable consumption. China has factored the precept into its Law on Protection of Consumer Rights and Interests. It has initiated educational and publicity programs. It has set up an eco-labeling scheme. It engages in certification of environmentally sound products. It has introduced a 30% reduction in sales tax for efficient cars. Its CO_2 emissions have been rising at a rate slower than expected. Similarly, Philippines has introduced taxes and fees on waste discharge and on resource consumption generally. India has developed one of the world's largest renewable energy programs.[22] Brazil has a green-labeling program, and it is promoting low- or noncarbon fuels such as biomass and hydropower. Russia has formed an Inter-Agency Commission on Climate Change. South Africa is vigorously promoting renewable energy and water efficiency. The developed countries, too, are taking sizeable steps. The European Union is to require recycling of up to 90% of electrical and electronic equipment, from PCs to dishwashers and from toys to cars.[23]

Eco-technologies are especially relevant to fossil fuels and ways to get more work out of every lump of coal, every drop of oil, and every whisp of natural gas. According to the American energy gurus Amory and Hunter Lovins, the United States alone could save as much as $300 billion per year through energy efficiency.[24] The rest of the industrialized world could probably save at least another $300 billion. Instead of economic pain through efforts to curb global warming, there would be profits aplenty. Yet certain U.S. politicians, notably President Bush, complain that efforts to cut back CO_2 emissions will hit both national economies and personal pockets. Hence President Bush has rejected the Kyoto Protocol with its proposals to reduce CO_2 emissions—even though his country, with less than 5% of the world's population, accounts for 25% of the world's emissions.

Alas that Bush and his supporters don't do their homework on energy economics. In 1973 when our good friends the Arabs taught us about the real price of oil, the United States and other industrialized countries began to show remarkable technological ingenuity in energy efficiency. They did it by obtaining the same mileage or lighting or heat with less energy than before and by using technologies that within a few months or years would pay for themselves. President Bush might note a statement by 2500 economists, including eight Nobel Prize winners: "For the United States, there are policy options that would slow climate change without harming American living standards, and these measures may in fact improve U.S. productivity in the longer run."[25] So if global warming turns out to be a fairy tale, the United States would still come out ahead thanks to money-making measures for energy efficiency. A win-win prospect indeed!

Fortunately American business is showing the way. IBM has reduced its energy use by 25% below its 1990 level, saving $527 million. DuPont has reduced its greenhouse gas (GHG) emissions by 45% and aims for 65% by 2010. Alcoa plans to reduce its GHG emissions by 2010 to 25% below 1990 levels. Similarly California aims to reduce electricity use by 10%. New York State plans to gain one-quarter of its electricity from carbon-free and renewable energy resources within a decade. Massachusetts has required six power plants to reduce their CO_2 emissions by 10% by 2007. New Jersey is to reduce its GHG emissions by 2005 to 3.5% below 1990 levels. More than 100 American cities have pledged to lower their GHG emissions. All this efficiency is underway even while the economy is expanding. How long will it take for the White House to feel the heat?

But note a key caveat. Eco-technologies themselves will not win the end game for us. We also need to curb our demand for products. Amory Lovins has devised a "hypercar" that will achieve 150 (possibly up to 300) kilometers per gallon, but if the fuel savings mean that consumers feel they can afford twice as many such cars, we shall be heading back to square one.

Conclusion

Will the day ever come when we shan't need to explain sustainable consumption, when it has become as much of an everyday term as sliced bread? Or when we hear the price of gasoline has gone up again, shall we throw a party to celebrate? How about this: "Have a sustainably nice day"?

CHAPTER IX

Sustainable Consumption: How to Get from Here to There

AND SO TO the final chapter, with a look into a revolutionary future where consumption is transformed from an activity "like there's no tomorrow" into a activity like there's endless tomorrows. It is not so much that current consumption is too high, rather it should be modified for certain areas such as food, energy, raw materials, and water, plus a lengthy shopping list (so to speak) of costly incidentals. To reiterate a pivotal point: what counts is not only quantity of livelihood but also quality of life.

Consider food, an item we consume several times a day. We have seen in chapter III that fast food leads to fast fat and can even end in fast death. Reader: when you've moved on from high-calorie meats, try eating locally. You'll enjoy food that is fresher, tastier, and healthier than food from afar. A typical meal item in the United States has traveled an average of at least 1500 kilometers before it reaches your dinner plate, one-quarter farther than in 1980. If the full cost of all those fossil fuels for transportation, including their pollution costs, were added onto the supermarket price, a California lettuce on a New Yorker's table would require tens of times as much fossil-fuel energy as it provides in food energy.[1] And why not enjoy the variety of seasonal fruits and veggies? Or couldn't we live without strawberries in February?

Consider the cautionary tale of a carton of strawberry yogurt marketed as "Made in Stuttgart" in southern Germany. The strawberries originate from Poland, whereupon they combine with yogurt from north Germany, jam from west Germany, sugar beet from France, and corn and wheat flour from the Netherlands. Only the milk and carton are produced in Stuttgart.[2] During the last 40 years while population has doubled, the value of international trade in food has tripled, and the weight of food shipped between countries has quadrupled.[3]

By contrast, note the explosive growth of farmers markets, being weekly gatherings when local consumers buy directly from local farmers. Money spent at these markets stays within the community, cycling through to create jobs and raise incomes as well as to support smallholder farmers. Every $10 spent at a farmers market is worth $25 for the local area, compared with $14 when it is spent in a supermarket. Such markets in the United States have grown from nearly 300 in the mid-1970s to well over 10 times as many today. Some three million people visit these markets each week and spend more than $1 billion each year. Since the mid-1970s, too, the global retail market for organic produce has jumped by three-quarters to reach $18 billion derived from 170,000 square kilometers of organically managed farmland, an expanse equivalent to Florida.[4]

Making a Personal Difference

What shall we do about runaway consumption? While this book addresses those people who are mainly enjoying grandscale consumption for the first time, they will be reluctant to do anything different until the long-rich people change gear. Let's look, then, at what that superconsumer society, America, could consider. The same applies of course to other highly consumerist societies (though not on the scale of America's), such as Britain, Germany, Japan, and the lengthy like.

Every American can make that famous difference, supposing he or she is one of the two out of three who say they would do more to conserve energy and protect the environment in dozens of other ways if they felt their individual actions would make a worthwhile impact.[5]

They must slay the dragon of rampant overconsumption—or at least put the dragon on a diet. Every last citizen can help, and every last one is needed like crazy. Here's how.

Make a start by introducing a few personal adjustments to your lifestyle. Even a single adjustment can make a notable difference. Skip one 30-kilometer car trip each week by telecommuting, biking, or combining errands, whereupon you will reduce your annual CO_2 emissions by half a tonne—and save at least $130. Replace one beef meal a week and thereby save more than 30 kilograms of grain and 40,000 gallons of water a year—as well as putting another $75 into your pocket. Reduce household electricity by replacing traditional light bulbs with energy-efficient fluorescent bulbs and moving the thermostat a few degrees Fahrenheit down in winter and up in summer, thus preventing well over 1 tonne of CO_2 emissions annually—and saving $165 a year. Install efficient showerheads and low-flow faucet aerators, and the household avoids more than 30,000 gallons of water and prevents 800 kilograms of CO_2 emissions each year—plus saving $50. Total saved per year: $425. If a family undertook a list of other similar actions as set out by the Center for a New American Dream's "Turn the Tide" program, (www.newdream.org/turnthetide), they would save enough to pay for a year-end vacation.[6]

Finally, inspire two friends to join you with these simple activities, and then get them to persuade two others in turn, and so on. If they all managed this every day (okay, a bit much), they would reach the entire United States within a month or so.

Next, consider something you can probably do every day, and again with sizeable clout. Shop carefully, and thus use your dollar votes to support the good-guy manufacturers, being the ones who try to be efficient with raw materials, who don't overexploit scarce natural resources, who aim for cradle-to-cradle products, who are miserly with energy, who plan for products manufactured with zero emissions, and all the other things that please Planet Earth. How do you learn which manufacturers are on the side of the angels? Check www.responsible-shopper.org or www.buygreen.com. Or if you are religious, take a look at "The Responsible Purchasing Guide for Faith Communities" (www.newdream.org/faith). Or you could try *Shopping for a Better World* from the Council for Economic Priorities in New York. Then too there is Vicki Robin's *Your Money or Your Life* at the New Road Map Foundation (www.newroadmap.org). Perhaps best of all is to check your own eco-footprint by consulting the website of Redefining Progress at www.rprogress.org.

Go for it—and remember that you live not only in a political democracy but an economic democracy too, the second allowing you to vote several times each day. Recall as well that if you don't go for it, you are unwittingly but effectively voting for the same dysfunctional world we are stuck with right now. Let's change it with every dollar bill.

Don't be surprised to find that as you do your bit to change the world, your actions are changing you. A big bonus of getting on with the task is that it will save you from that dread sense of paralysis in face of proliferant problems on every side. In addition to the shopping list of antishopping items that the counterconsumption crusader will readily think up, make yourself a promise that once a year you will plant a tree. True, if a million people were to do as much, it would not soak up enough carbon dioxide to make a difference to global warming. But it will make a difference to the way you feel about yourself. Go and dig in the ground, get your hands dirty, offer long life to a sapling, and you'll be registering a vote for yourself as well as the planet.

Or keep on recalling the protester who was told by the politician that carrying a placard would not make the politician become like him. "No," came the response, "but it will stop me becoming like you."

How else to make your difference? You could try your hand at volunteer work to support the environment or to otherwise offset your lifestyle impacts (nobody treads the planet with zero impact). In the Netherlands the work of volunteers equals 450,000 full-time jobs— and that in a country with a labor force of only six million. These activities are worth around $14 billion a year, or almost $1000 per citizen.

In South Korea—a new-consumer country—nearly four million people volunteer more than 450 million hours per year, worth more than $2 billion, or $40 per citizen. In Brazil—another new-consumer country—at least one adult in six volunteers some part of his or her free time.[7] If you want to join the band, check www.parti.org/how-you-can-help/volunteer.com. On December 5 each year, designated the International Volunteer Day, you can seek out a rallying point for organizations and individuals to express support for the Millennium Development Goals, in which environmental activities are prominent.[8] Of if you want to go straight to organizations that recruit volunteers for the environment, try the World Wildlife Fund, Earthwatch, Raleigh International, Greenforce, or the David Suzuki Foundation.

If you feel you want to do still more, consider a grand strategy known as voluntary simplicity.[9] In popular parlance it is often referred to as downshifting, or shifting to a more simple and relaxed, albeit less affluent, lifestyle; in other words, leaving the rat race to those sleek overcompetitive rats.[10] Way back in the early 1990s millions of American workers, including every tenth executive or professional, went to their employers and said they would like to work fewer hours, and of course they would take home less pay. They could then spend more time with their spouses, children, friends, and neighbors, and they could enjoy more time on a martini or a sunset. Many of them liked it so much that next year they went back to their employers and requested still fewer hours at work.[11] For sure, they still total a small share of the U.S. populace. But then, those Americans who struggled for civil rights or an end to the Vietnam War once numbered only a small share of all Americans.

The same is happening in Britain where millions of people have given up well-paid jobs as a rejection of the "culture of endless getting and spending," despite increasing pressures to earn and spend more.[12] In mid-2003 a senior government minister became the third top-flight official to abandon a highly promising career (he was viewed as a potential prime minister) to spend more time with his family.

Want to know more about the voluntary simplicity movement? Try organizations and publications such as Real Simple, Live Simple, the Simply Living Network, the Frugality Network, the Center for a New American Dream, Alternatives for Simple Living, the *Simple Living Resource Guide*, the Simple Family Life, the Lifestyle Movement, Simple Abundance, Fringe Wisdom, Living and Having More with Less, Living without a Car, Voluntary Simplicity Overview, or the *Journal of Voluntary Simplicity*.

Voluntary simplicity ranks high among many of the people known as "cultural creatives." There are 50 million of them in the United States, every fourth adult, and even more of them in Europe where they make up every third adult. They espouse strong environmental viewpoints, they highlight relationships, they are generally committed to psychological development and even spirituality, they are turned off by large institutions (including both the extreme left and right in politics), and above all they reject conspicuous consumption. They focus on renewable energy and resource-efficient products, alternative transportation, nature protection, organic products, alternative health care, socially responsible investments, eco-tourism, and lifelong education. They watch only half as much television but listen to twice as much radio as does the general public; they read as many books as magazines; and they are Internet addicts. They include the 30 million Americans who practice yoga, up from 4 million in 1990. Two-thirds of the cultural creatives are women, and they walk their talk.[13]

The Auroville Experiment

What, dear reader, are you saying that despite all the above, human nature cannot change? That people are, on the whole, hardwired to want more and waste more and that consumption patterns are set in concrete? Well, note that in the recent past at least 60 million Americans have given up smoking. At the start of the period they were under social pressure to light up, and at the end of it they were under social pressure to stub out. It has been a cultural earthquake, almost overnight.

You may still respond that this is an isolated item and says nothing about the bigger picture. Consider a community in southern India that has foresworn consumption from top to bottom. Auroville, meaning "city of the dawn," is a highly innovative community, as this book's first author has invariably noted on his repeated visits there (where he served on the International Advisory Committee) (www.auroville. org). Started in 1968, it contains 1500 residents, 500 of them Indians and the rest from 40 countries around the world. Their eventual aim is to build up to 50,000 members. They are not hippy-type "do nothings"; they are mostly educated and enterprising people bent on making their planet-saving lifestyles function in the Monday-morning world. When the first pioneers arrived, they were armed with little more than their ideals for a new model of life on Earth, centered on simplified living, self-reliance and environmental know-how. They could hardly have been assigned a more unpromising place. They were allotted 10 square kilometers of land so degraded that it was officially declared "unfit for human habitation." There were only a few dozen trees, there were scant streams and no rivers, and there was next to no topsoil. Today the soil cover has been restored, rivers flourish, and there are two million trees.

Auroville's agriculture supplies half of its food while depending on organic fertilizers and pesticides. The community uses solar and wind power for much of its energy. It employs photovoltaics to supply electricity to light buildings, to pump and heat water, and to cook food. The township's use of solar energy in so profitable that it has become a demonstration model for the whole of India. It exploits wind power too, through several dozen windmills, some of which pump water from 30 meters down. In addition, Aurovilleans are pioneers in eco-technologies for water reclamation, agroforestry, soil conservation, and land rehabilitation.

In still more striking ways, Auroville's lifestyles epitomize the goal of "living lightly on the face of the planet." Members agree to a cash income of only $100 per month, together with subsidized food, housing, water, clothing, and other basic needs, plus permanent employment, worth $250 per month. This makes a total of little over $4000 per year. Simple living with a vengeance, and with endless satisfaction—as I have witnessed during my frequent sojourns onsite.

Bottom line: it is Auroville's philosophy as well as its eco-technologies that make the system work. To cite the late prime minister of India, Indira Gandhi, Auroville is "an exciting project for understanding the environmental needs for people's spiritual growth."[14] Auroville's vision is an ambitious goal—and one that is essential if the world's communities are to live in a way that suggests they plan to remain on Earth forever rather than act as visitors for a weekend.

The Biggest Question

This book has raised many questions about where we are now, where we want to go, and how we get from here to there. Now for the biggest question of all: what do we truly want from consumption, and is it delivering?

The answer might seem so obvious that it is not worth stating. Hundreds of millions of people proclaim the consumerist message through their actions every day of their lives, and many more want to join the throng. Politicians of every sort and stripe, in every land, view it as what every voter wants above all else. The marketplace urges it as a glorious given. To question it suggests the questioner comes from outer space.

And yet, and yet. There are murmurings if not rumblings in many a quarter to the effect that consumption as generally practiced may not always be up to its job. Perhaps, just conceivably, we are sometimes confusing means with ends. We pursue consumption to make our lives better: that is its clear purpose. It has become so widespread and deep-seated that it is squeezing out any other means of achieving the ultimate purpose. To question it is not just heresy, it is nonsense. It is to close one's eyes to the way the world works, to what makes individuals tick.

Let us take a big deep breath and ask if the end invariably justifies the means. In fact there are quite a few people taking that breath, and they are not idle layabouts, they are some of the brightest and best among us. There is an emergent trend in the long-rich countries whereby certain people are increasingly asking if greater wealth, whether of the economy or the citizen, must inevitably lead to greater well-being. There is evidence a-building in the United States and Europe that the road to riches is far from a necessary road to fulfilment—or, if we dare to use a big word, happiness. If there is any substance to this line of thinking, it might prompt the new consumers to pause and consider the upshot of endless consumption.

Many people sense that consumption gives them a fine feeling in the right place, so ever-more consumption should give them ever-greater happiness. But does it? Absurd as this question may have sounded a few years ago, it is gaining a hearing in many quarters. Whereas the British economist guru John Keynes once asserted that consumption is the primary purpose of humankind, there are cold-eyed economists today who contest this in certain respects. They include Nobel Prize–winner Daniel Kahneman,[15] Richard Layard of the London School of Economics,[16] and many other economists in the boom industry of what is known in the trade as happiness research. The new view is even gaining attention from top-level officialdom. The British government has recently published a report on life satisfaction with hints that personal fulfilment may soon become "the new money." Already there is a pioneering effort on the part of a little country with big ideas, Bhutan in the Himalayas. Its government looks beyond Gross National Income to assess Gross National Happiness, based on the four principles of economic development, environmental protection, cultural promotion, and good governance—all to be sustainable.[17]

In sum, happiness is not simply a peaches and cream affair. After all, people who run marathons (no minority sport) may not feel much conventional pleasure, but they sense satisfaction so deep that they can hardly find it elsewhere. But what "real world" evidence is there to support the idea that consumption is less than a never-ending pleasure trip? It seems that when people reach an individual income level of around $10,000 a year, being enough to meet their basic material needs, they find that more income does not always lead to more happiness in the sense of lifestyle fulfilment.[18] During the last half century people in rich countries have not only become much more affluent but they are healthier, they live longer, they work less, and they travel more widely on longer vacations. Yet they feel they are no happier. Consider, for instance, how rushed and frazzled we have become. Technocrats have brought us one time-saving device after another, notably washing machines, clothes driers, microwave ovens, blenders, and push-button phones among a host of such items. Despite the time that these items have saved, we now find ourselves with less of "our" time than before.[19] Not even enough time to sleep; a morning rush-hour train or bus can be full of passengers snoozing. Many business people commute for more than an hour at each end of the day, never seeing their children awake throughout the working week. Some of them are starting to say they would prefer more sleep to more salary.[20]

Recent research shows that only one-third of Americans feel "very happy," no more than in 1950.[21] During much the same period, Britons have achieved twice as much income in real terms, yet their perceived quality of life has not increased; two-thirds of them would rather see the environment improve than have more economic growth and personal spending money.[22] In fact, a "happiness index" places Britain 32nd and the United States 46th out of 54 countries assessed, ranked behind such "poor" countries as China and Philippines.[23] In Europe generally, there has been no long-term rise in happiness except in Italy and Denmark. Japan features no change in its low level of happiness despite a sixfold increase in per-capita income in just three decades.[24] Most new consumers in Russia sense frustration with their supposed well-being.[25]

To this extent, affluence appears to be far from the answer to all problems. What people most want is a lifestyle with solid satisfaction through things like personal relationships, good health, and valued work.[26] Indeed, many people say they suffer from a kind of psychic and emotional poverty, largely due to excessive and misplaced consumerism, plus community decline and environmental rundown.[27] To cite Dr. Laurie Michaelis, of the former Oxford Commission on Sustainable Consumption, "Consumption is about belonging with other people, not being better than other people. Belonging is what people are really hungry for. Once basic material needs are met, what really makes people happy are decent relationships or an interesting job."[28]

This line of thinking could be what lies behind an even more heretical notion—that many people enjoy consumption primarily when it is conspicuous consumption and a source of personal prestige, whereupon they often find it brings outer contentment but at a cost of inner satisfaction.[29] It is "keep up with the Jones's" again, or even "keep ahead of the Jones's." As Will Rogers once said, many people spend money they don't have on things they don't want in order to impress people they don't like.

Such consumers can also suffer from the stress of overmany possessions, together with debt and waste. The number of individuals in Britain declaring themselves bankrupt has topped 100 people a day at a time when personal borrowing continues to surge at record speed. The proportion of these bankruptcies due to consumer debt has risen by two-thirds in the past eight years.[30] Despite the highest income levels ever known in Britain, well over half of all citizens feel depressed periodically. These people are twice as likely to say they sometimes buy things that they later regret.[31] In fact, people whose values center on material goods seem to face a greater risk of depression, a reaction that applies regardless of age, income, or culture.[32] Despite the all-singing advertisers in Britain who suggest that consumers are one big happy family, well over half of citizens are depressed from time to time, ostensibly because they buy things they cannot afford and things that often fail to supply satisfaction.[33] In high-income countries, depression now ranks second in the world table of diseases, more widespread than cancer. Yet depression drives many sufferers to seek retail therapy at the shopping mall. Materialism causes unhappiness, and unhappiness causes materialism.[34]

Here's still more evidence. In Britain three-fifths of people say they cannot afford to buy everything they really need, yet almost 9 out of 10 people think British society is "too materialistic [with] too much emphasis on money and not enough on the things that really matter."[35] In the top two income brackets, 4 people in 10 say that if they had a choice, they would take more vacation rather than a pay raise. Nearly the same number want to spend more time with family and friends, while almost 3 in 10 want to enjoy nature more. Only 1 in 7, mainly young people, say that a greater priority lies with shopping. This contrasts strongly with the image of a modern world peopled by couch potatoes and television addicts. Only 1 British person in 50 wants to be remembered as wealthy and materially successful.[36] Who on their death bed wishes they had earned more in order to consumer more?

All this reflects, of course, the consumption pressures of the rich countries, with societies that have long exceeded the bounds of acceptable consumption. For them consumption has often spilled over into mis- and overconsumption. The new consumers for the most part have yet to reach that stage, with the exception of their emphasis on meat-based diets and ever-more cars. They might take heed, however, of the insidious allurements of consumption for its own self-consuming sake.

Beyond Today's Consumption

A final question arises, stemming from the backlash effects of runaway consumption. Could we be on the verge of one of the greatest revolutions in human history, when people leave behind 10,000 years of fixation on all-out consumption and shift their lifestyle priorities to something different and better? With over-the-top consumption out of the way, people would have space to try out new this and sample fresh that. It would amount to a big exploration, a huge adventure.

It would be a seismic shift, and virtually instantaneous within human history—a shift in spending, a shift in thinking. It could rank as one of the biggest shifts ever. However hard it may be to envision at this stage, recall the management guru Peter Drucker's words, albeit with reference to humankind's planetary impact writ large: "Every few hundred years in Western history there occurs a sharp transformation. Within a few short decades, society rearranges itself—its world view, its basic values, its social and political structure, its arts, its key institutions. We are currently living through such a transformation."[37]

Not that the transformation would mean an end to consumption. Quite the opposite. It would mean an advance to consumption of a basically different sort, what we might call "consumption of knowledge and experience." Thus far we have mainly contented ourselves with the manufactured products of industry, notably cars, washing machines, fridges, houses. All these can be consumed by only one individual or household at a time, and they are used until they are used up. Nobody else shares in their consumption (which is part of their appeal). By contrast, the "new consumption" would focus on "knowledge products" such as sports, the arts, outdoors trips, and exploratory travel. These can be not only consumed but possessed and shared with many other consumers. Compare, for instance, a car to a concert, whether classical or pop. The car can be owned, whereupon its enjoyment is denied to others (who may actually lose through road congestion and traffic pollution). Conversely all knowledge products, which are fortunately multiplying in kinds and numbers, can be copied many times over. They can be enjoyed by consumers without end, and they remain available for future consumption without end.[38]

Suppose, however, that a shift to knowledge products rather than material goods meant a shift in the economy. It need not mean an end to the ever-growing economy, rather an end to the economy that we have known. Knowledge products have their role in the marketplace, making for an economy akin in some ways to the service economy that in many countries is displacing the material-goods economy. In any case, the growth economy needs to give way to the "development economy" directed at human development, just as we do not need to grow the Earth in order to develop the Earth.

A shift to a sustainable form of consumption would be a revolution indeed. Daunting as may be the prospect, it is unavoidable if only for abundant environmental reasons. We shall undertake the change either by default or by design. But the revolution will run up against a profound trait of our species: resistance to change. It is not that we don't like change, it is rather that we don't like things to be different. To cite a perceptive observer, Sir Crispin Tickell: "It takes time to learn to think differently. If policy lags behind change of mind, and practice behind policy, little will change unless and until we think differently. The power of inertia is immensely strong, especially in the functioning engine room of society—the middle ranks—whether in government, business or elsewhere. For change we need three factors: leadership from above, pressure from below, or some exemplary catastrophe."[39]

We live in a time of change anyway: change on every side, change without parallel in history, and change that will leave our futures unrecognizable. The world is changing outasight, and what is changing most is the speed of change. Yet one thing does not seem to have changed much, and that is our capacity to recognize change. For instance, when we make our way to our workplaces each day, do we sense that we are traveling through an atmosphere that is changing climatically more than in 100,000 years? We can't see the change, we can't smell it, we can't taste it, even though it is one of the most potent forces in our world. Yesterday the world's population increased by one-quarter of a million people, as much as would have taken almost two weeks in 1900: who of us could tell the difference? We seem to be programmed to dismiss change, to tune it out. "I've smoked for thirty years, so what harm will another year do?"—even though we know that sooner or later that extra year could mark a terminal change. Recall the man who fell out of a twentieth storey window, and said as he passed the tenth floor, "Nothing new so far."

How to set about the consumption challenge, being one of the biggest changes that human societies have ever encountered? If it doesn't bear thinking about, it therefore demands a great deal of thinking. Fortunately, and as we have seen in this book, there are experts aplenty who believe we can do it. Whether we will actually do it—whether we will devise the eco-technologies, make the philosophic shifts, and so on, backed by the right public opinion and political leadership—is another matter. We may find that the most valuable resource, and the one in shortest supply, will be our willingness to change our understanding of how best to live on our limited planet. If we feel daunted by this supersize prospect, we should bear in mind (again) that we do not face a choice between change and no change. Rather it is between change that we choose or change that we suffer as a result of nonchoice. Shall we choose to choose?

Clincher factor: however hard it will be to live with the profound changes ahead, it will not be so hard as to live in a world profoundly impoverished by the environmental devastation of current consumption. The question is not "can we afford to consume sustainably?" Rather it is "how can we afford not to?" Let us bear in mind the insight of the leader of the Rio Earth Summit, Maurice Strong: "History demonstrates that what seems unrealistic today becomes inevitable tomorrow."[40]

Sign-off thought: could the time come when we shall hail the country that, by leading the way to the New Consumption, has become a lifestyle leader—or even a lifestyle superpower?

GNI and Its Shortcomings

In chapter 1 we have looked at the new consumers within the context of per-capita Gross National Income (GNI), reckoned in PPP terms. The concept of GNI is central to the calculations. As we have seen, it is a device for measuring the economic value of all goods and services produced in a country. In turn, per-capita GNI serves as a very rough indicator of how all the country's citizens are faring. But there are problems with the concept, as with its implications for new-consumer numbers.

The first is that GNI is only a crude and indirect measure of personal affluence since it reflects the entire economy rather than individual citizens' purchasing power. In fact the second is often only around two-thirds of the first because national economies include a lot of public goods and services such as capital stocks, infrastructure, and other factors. Secondly, GNI does not reflect many economic activities and values that lie outside the marketplace. It says much about quantity of livelihood, little about quality of life such as environment, health, leisure, and security. Thirdly, GNI does not reflect the many marketplace activities that lie outside the official economy, these underground activities including tax evasion, trade in stolen goods and drugs, clandestine gambling, fraud, prostitution and a host of other illicit doings.[1] In a good number of countries (including the United States) they amount to no more than 10% of GNI, though in India the unofficial economy may be 30% as large as the official economy, and in Russia it is now estimated to be as much as one-half,[2] with many new consumers earning their wealth through black markets.

A fourth qualifier of GNI as a key indicator of new consumerdom is that many countries engage in hefty government subsidies. China has been subsidizing basic needs to the extent that only a small part of household income has been going to food, health, education, rent, and transportation, meaning that Chinese households have more spending power than their incomes would lead an outsider to suppose.[3]

Finally, note that national income is not the same as personal income, nor is personal income always the same as personal consumption. Some people save a good part of their earnings, others do not. Most developed-country citizens save at least 10–20% of their incomes, but Americans save hardly anything (many are even in permanent debt). For present purposes, let us assume that most new consumers want to enjoy the full fruits of their earnings, so savings do not significantly reduce their consumer spending. To this extent, household income and consumption can be taken to mean roughly the same thing.

Four Outlier Countries

There is a further wrinkle to the assessment. Four of the twenty countries—South Korea, Mexico, Turkey, and Poland—are members of the Organization for Economic Cooperation and Development (OECD), the "rich nations club," even though their per capita GNIs are far below those of the 23 long-standing high-income OECD members. Their per capita GNIs in 2002 were PPP$16,480, 8540, 6120, and 10,130 respectively, by contrast with an average for the 23 OECD countries of PPP$27,600, and with an average for developing countries of around PPP$3600. The four countries have been listed in World Bank and United Nations documents as "middle income" or "upper middle income" countries (as opposed to "rich" countries of the developed world), hence they are included here as developing or transition countries insofar as they have some way to go before they match the affluence of the principal OECD countries.

Notes

Chapter I

1. A. Smith, *An Inquiry into the Nature and Causes of the Wealth of Nations* (www.adamsmith.org/smith/won-intro.htm) (1976).

2. A. Durning, "Asking How Much is Enough," in L. R. Brown et al., *The State of the World 1991* (New York: Norton, 1991), 153–169; see also D. Bloom, S. Radelet, T. Panayotou, A. Warren, J. Williamson, and J. Sachs, *Emerging Asia* (Manila: Asian Development Bank, 1997); J. E. Garten, *The Big Ten: The Big Emerging Markets and How They Will Change Our Lives* (New York: Basic Books, 1997); H. Henderson, "Looking Back from the 21st Century," *Futures Research Quarterly* 13(3) (1997): 83–98; G. Pauli, *Upsizing: The Road to Zero Emissions, More Jobs, More Income and No Pollution* (Sheffield, UK: Greenleaf Publishing, 1998); J. Sachs, *The Geography of Global Capitalism* (Cambridge, MA: Harvard Institute for International Development, 1997).

3. P. R. Ehrlich and A. H. Ehrlich, *One with Nineveh: Politics, Consumption and the Human Future* (Washington, DC: Island Press, 2004); R. B. Heap and J. Kent, *Towards Sustainable Consumption: A European Perspective* (London: The Royal Society, 2000); N. Myers and J. Kent, "New Consumers: The Influence of Affluence on the Environment," *Proceedings of the National Academy of Sciences* (USA) 100 (2003): 4963–4968; T. Princen, M. Maniates, and K. Conca, eds., *Confronting Consumption* (Cambridge, MA: MIT Press, 2002); P. C. Stern, T. Dietz, V. W Ruttan, R. H. Socolow, and J. L Sweeney, eds., *Environmentally Significant Consumption: Research Directions* (Washington, DC: National Academy Press, 1997).

4. P. H. Gleick, "Water and Conflict," in P. H. Gleick, *The World's Water 1998–1999* (Washington, DC: Island Press, 1998), 105–135; M. T. Klare, *Resource Wars: The New Landscape of Global Conflict* (New York: Henry Holt, 2001); S. L. Postel and A. T. Wolf, "Dehydrating Conflict," *Foreign Policy*, September 2001, 2–9; M. Renner, *The Anatomy of Resource Wars* (Washington, DC: Worldwatch Institute, 2002).

5. M. Wackernagel et al., "Tracking the Ecological Overshoot of the Human Economy," *Proceedings of National Academy of Sciences* (USA) 99 (2002): 9266–9271.

6. World Resources Institute, *World Resources 2000–2001* (Washington, DC: World Resources Institute, 2000); see also United Nations Development Programme, *Human Development Report 2001* (New York: Oxford University Press, 2001).

7. United Nations Development Programme, *Human Development Report 1998* (New York: Oxford University Press, 1998).

8. K. Rogoff, "The Purchasing Power Parity Puzzle," *Journal of Economic Literature* 34 (1996): 647–668.

9. World Bank, *World Development Indicators 2003* (www.worldbank.org/data/wdi2003/).

10. Garten, *The Big Ten: The Big Emerging Markets and How They Will Change Our Lives;* N. Robins and S. Roberts, "Making Sense of Sustainable Consumption," *Development* 41 (1998): 28–36; J. Rohwer, *Asia Rising: How History's Biggest Middle Class Will Change the World* (London: Nicholas Brealey, 1996).

11. International Energy Agency, *International Energy Outlook 2000* (Paris: IEA, 2000); L. Schipper, C. Marie-Lilliu, and G. Lewis-Davis, *Rapid Motorization in the Largest Countries in Asia: Implications for Oil, Carbon Dioxide and Transportation* (Paris: International Energy Agency, 1999).

12. World Bank, *World Development Indicators 2003* (www.worldbank.org/data/wdi2003/).

13. World Bank, *World Development Report 1994* (New York: Oxford University Press, 1994); World Bank, *World Development Indicators 2003* (www.worldbank.org/data/wdi2003/).

14. Myers and Kent, "New Consumers: The Influence of Affluence on the Environment."

15. J. J. McCusker, "How Much Is That Worth Today?: Comparing the Purchasing Power of Money in Great Britain from 1264 to 2002" (www.eh.net/hmit/ppowerbp/) (2001).

16. N. Kristof and S. WuDunn, *Thunder from the East: Portrait of a Rising Asia* (New York: Knopf, 2000); E. Galeno, *Paradoxes* (New York: Znet, 2002).

17. Tata Energy Research Institute, *Growth of Motor Vehicles Registered in India* (New Delhi: TERI, 2003).

18. V. Melkova, "Russian Middle Class Hits 25%," *The Russia Journal*, February 3, 2001 (www.therussiajournal.com/index. htm?obj=4158).

19. World Bank, *World Development Indicators 2003* (www.worldbank.org/ data/wdi2003/).

20. Energy Information Administration International Energy Database (www.eia.doe.gov/emeu/international/contents.html) (2003).

21. "The Economists' Statement on Climate Change," endorsed by more than 2500 economists including eight Nobel Laureates (for a summary see www.rprogress.org/publications/econstatement.html); Inter-Academy Panel, "Transition to Sustainability in the 21st Century: The Contribution of Science and Technology" (www4.nas.edu/iap/ iaphome.nsf/weblinks/SAIN-4XVLCT?OpenDocument) (2000); Union of Concerned Scientists, *World Scientists' Warning to Humanity* (Cambridge, MA: Union of Concerned Scientists, 1992); National Academy of Sciences (USA) and Royal Society (London) *Population Growth, Resource Consumption, and a Sustainable World* (Washington DC and London: National Academy of Sciences and Royal Society, 1992).

22. R. Costanza et al., "The Value of the World's Ecosystem Services and Natural Capital," *Nature* 387 (1997): 253–260.

23. P. Hawken, "Natural Capitalism," *Mother Jones* (March/April 1997): 40–54; see also L. R. Brown et al., *State of the World 1999* (New York: Norton, 1999); P. Hawken, A. B. Lovins, and L. H. Lovins *Natural Capitalism* (Boston: Little, Brown, 1999); E. von Weizsacker, A. B. Lovins, and L. H. Lovins, *Factor Four: Doubling Wealth, Halving Resource Use* (London: Earthscan, 1997).

24. Ministry of Environment (Norway), *Symposium: Sustainable Consumption* (Oslo: Ministry of Environment, 1994); see also I. Christie and D. Warburton, *From Here to Sustainability* (London: Earthscan, 2001); H. E. Daly, *Ecological Economics and the Ecology of Economics: Essays in Criticism* (Cheltenham, UK: Edward Elgar, 2000); Heap and Kent, "Towards Sustainable Consumption: A European Perspective"; T. Prugh, R. Costanza, and H. Daly, *The Local Politics of Global Sustainability* (Washington, DC: Island Press, 2000); R. N. Stavins, ed. *Economics of the Environment: Selected Readings* (New York: Norton, 2000).

Chapter II

1. G. K. Ingram and Z. Liu, *Motorization and the Provision of Roads in Countries and Cities* (Washington, DC: The World Bank, 1997); International Energy Agency, *International Energy Outlook 2000* (Paris: IEA, 2000); L. Schipper, C. Marie-Lilliu, and G. Lewis-Davis, *Rapid Motorization in the Largest Countries in Asia: Implications for Oil, Carbon Dioxide and Transportation* (Paris: International Energy Agency, 1999).

2. United Nations Development Programme, *Human Development Report 1998* (New York: Oxford University Press, 1998).

3. World Bank, *World Development Indicators 2003* (www.worldbank.org/ data/wdi2003/).

4. J. Abrenica, "The Asian Automotive Industry," *Asian-Pacific Economic Literature* 12(1) (1998): 12–26; Consumers International Regional Office for Asia and the Pacific, *A Discerning Middle Class? A Preliminary Enquiry of Sustainable Consumption Trends in Selected Countries in the Asia Pacific Region* (Penang, Malaysia: Consumers International Regional Office for Asia and the Pacific [CI- ROAP], 1998); L. E. Smith, letter, *Ward's Communications*, March 10, 2000.

5. Energy Information Administration, *International Energy Outlook 2001* (Washington, DC: U.S. Department of Energy, 2001).

6. L. Aron, "In Search of a Russian Middle Class," *Russian Outlook* (Fall) (Washington, DC: American Enterprise Institute for Public Policy Research, 2000).

7. World Bank, *World Development Indicators 2003* (www.worldbank.org/ data/wdi2003/); L. R. Brown et al., *Vital Signs 1999* (New York: Norton, 1999); R. Priddle, *The Meaning of Kyoto* (Paris: International Energy Agency, 1998).

8. Smith, letter, *Ward's Communications;* World Bank, *World Development Indicators 2003* (www.worldbank.org/data/wdi2003/); World Resources Institute, *Critical Consumption Trends and Implications: Degrading Earth's Ecosystems* (Washington, DC: World Resources Institute, 1999).

9. Schipper et al, *Rapid Motorization in the Largest Countries in Asia: Implications for Oil, Carbon Dioxide and Transportation.*

10. Ibid.

11. N. Myers and J. Kent, "New Consumers: The Influence of Affluence on the Environment," *Proceedings of the National Academy of Sciences* (USA) 100 (2003): 4963–4968.

12. Schipper et al, *Rapid Motorization in the Largest Countries in Asia: Implications for Oil, Carbon Dioxide and Transportation.*

13. World Bank, *World Development Indicators 2003* (www.worldbank.org/data/wdi2003/); Smith, letter, *Ward's Communications*.

14. World Bank, *World Development Indicators 2003* (www.worldbank.org/data/wdi2003/).

15. L. R. Brown et al, *State of the World 2001* (New York: Norton, 2001); Organization for Economic Cooperation and Development, *Sustainable Consumption and Production* (Paris: OECD, 1997); M. M. Sheehan, *City Limits: Putting the Brakes on Sprawl* (Washington, DC: Worldwatch Institute, 2001).

16. C. Willoughby, *Managing Motorization* (Washington, DC: Transport Division, The World Bank, 2000).

17. International Energy Agency, *International Energy Outlook 2000*.

18. P. DuPont and K. Egan, "Solving Bangkok's Transport Woes: The Need to Ask the Right Questions," *World Transport and Policy Practice* 3(1) (1997): 25–37; World Health Organization, *Health and Environment in Sustainable Development: Five Years After the Earth Summit* (Geneva: WHO, 1997).

19. C. Brandon and K. Homman, *The Cost of Inaction: Valuing the Economy-Wide Cost of Environmental Degradation in India* (New Delhi: The World Bank, 1995).

20. A. Agarwal and S. Narain, *Economic Globalisation: Its Impact on Consumption, Equity and Sustainability* (New Delhi: Center for Science and the Environment, 1997); Brandon and Homman, *The Cost of Inaction: Valuing the Economy-Wide Cost of Environmental Degradation in India;* W. W. Gibbs, "Transportation's Perennial Problems," *Scientific American* 277(4) (1997): 54–57.

21. D. Sperling and E. Clausen, "The Developing World's Motorization Challenge," *Issues in Science and Technology* 19(1) (2002): 59–66.

22. R. E Weisbrod, "Solving China's Urban Crisis: China's Transportation Energy Future," *Journal of Urban Technology* 6 (1999): 89–100; Zhou Fengqi, *Energy Consumption and Sustainable Development in China* (Beijing: Energy Research Institute, 1997).

23. United Nations Development Programme, *Human Development Report 1998*.

24. World Bank, *World Development Indicators 2003* (www.worldbank.org/data/wdi2003/).

25. R. M. DeSouza, *Household Transportation Use and Urban Air Pollution* (Washington, DC: Population Reference Bureau, 2001); United Nations Development Programme, *Human Development Report 1998;* World

Health Organization, *Health and Environment in Sustainable Development: Five Years After the Earth Summit.*

26. D. W. Pearce, "Benefit-Cost Analysis, Environment, and Health in the Developed and Developing World," *Environment and Development Economics* (1998): 210–214.

27. International Energy Agency, *International Energy Outlook 2002* (Paris: IEA, 2002).

28. World Health Organization, *Health and Environment in Sustainable Development: Five Years After the Earth Summit.*

29. A. Schafer and D. Victor, "The Past and Future of Global Mobility," *Scientific American* 277(4) (1997): 58–61.

30. United Nations Development Programme, *Human Development Report 1998.*

31. L. Schipper and C. Lilliu-Marie, *Transportation and CO$_2$ Emissions: Flexing the Link—A Path for the World Bank* (Washington, DC: The World Bank, 1999); United Nations Development Programme, *Human Development Report 1998.*

32. Energy Information Administration, *International Energy Outlook 2003* (Washington, DC: U.S. Department of Energy, 2003); see also Sperling and Clausen, "The Developing World's Motorization Challenge"; Organization for Economic Cooperation and Development, *Influencing Road Travel Demand: You Can't Reach Kyoto by Car* (Paris: OECD, 2001).

33. L. R. Brown, *Paving the Planet: Cars and Crops Competing for Land* (Washington, DC: Worldwatch Institute, 2001).

34. Sheehan, *City Limits: Putting the Brakes on Sprawl.*

35. A. B. Lovins and L. H. Lovins, "Fool's Gold in Alaska," *Foreign Affairs* 80(4) (2001): 72–85.

36. V. McGrane, *Pricing Driving Accurately* (San Francisco: Redefining Progress, 2001).

37. J. DeCicco and Feng An, *Automakers Corporate Carbon Budgets: Reframing Public Policy on Automobiles, Oil and Climate* (New York: Environmental Defense, 2002).

38. A. B. Lovins, *U.S. Energy Security Linked to Efficiency* (Snowmass, CO: Rocky Mountain Institute, 2003).

39. Energy Information Administration, *Transportation Energy Use* (Washington, DC: U.S. Department of Energy, 2002); V. McGrane, *Pricing Driving Accurately.*

40. A. B. Lovins, *Energy Security Facts: Details and Documentation* (Snowmass, CO: Rocky Mountain Institute, 2003) (www.rmi.org/sitepages/pid533.php#UsEnergySecFacts).

41. P. Angelides, "Announcing New Bill Eliminating Unnecessary Gas Guzzlers from State Fleet," news release (www.treasurer.ca.gov/news/releases/2003/20030612SUV) (2003; site now discontinued).

42. A. B. Lovins, *Hypercars: The Future* (Snowmass, CO: Rocky Mountain Institute, 1998).

43. R. T. T. Forman and D. Sperling, *Road Ecology: Science and Solutions* (Washington, DC: Island Press, 2003); L. Fulton, J. Hardy, L. Schipper, and A. Gulub, *Bus Systems for the Future: Achieving Sustainable Transport Worldwide* (Paris: International Energy Agency, 2002).

44. J. Lerner, *What Are Sustainable Communities? Case Study of Curitiba, Brazil* (Washington, DC: National Council for Science and the Environment, 2001); Sheehan, *City Limits: Putting the Brakes on Sprawl;* Sperling and Clausen, "The Developing World's Motorization Challenge."

45. Sheehan, *City Limits: Putting the Brakes on Sprawl;* Sperling and Clausen, "The Developing World's Motorization Challenge"; Fulton et al., *Bus Systems for the Future: Achieving Sustainable Transport Worldwide.*

46. Fulton et al., *Bus Systems for the Future: Achieving Sustainable Transport Worldwide;* Sperling and Clausen, "The Developing World's Motorization Challenge."

47. L. R. Brown and J. Larsen, *World Turning to Bicycle for Mobility and Exercise* (Washington, DC: Earth Policy Institute, 2002).

48. P. Newman and J. Kenworthy, *Sustainability and Cities: Overcoming Automobile Dependence* (Washington, DC: Island Press, 1999); Sheehan, *City Limits: Putting the Brakes on Sprawl.*

49. Sperling and Clausen, "The Developing World's Motorization Challenge."

50. Worldwatch Institute, *Vital Signs 2002* (New York: Norton, 2002).

51. Forman and Sperling, *Road Ecology: Science and Solutions.*

52. T. Litman, *Socially Optimal Transport Prices and Markets* (Victoria, Canada: Victoria Transport Policy Institute, 1999).

53. Energy Information Administration, *Transportation Energy Use.*

54. J. Motavalli, *Forward Drive: The Race to Build Clean Cars for the Future* (London: Earthscan, 2002).

55. S. Dunn, *Hydrogen Futures: Toward a Sustainable Energy System* (Washington, DC: Worldwatch Institute, 2001).

56. M. I. Hoffert et al., "Advanced Technology Paths to Global Climate Stability: Energy for a Greenhouse Planet," *Science* 298 (2002): 981–987.

57. M. Renner, "Vehicle Production Declines Slightly," in Worldwatch Institute, *Vital Signs 2002* (New York: Norton, 2002), 74–75.

58. Motavalli, *Forward Drive: The Race to Build Clean Cars for the Future.*

59. United Nations Environment Programme, *Marketing "Cool" Life-styles Key to Selling Clean and Green Products* (Nairobi: UNEP, 2003); United Nations Environment Programme, *Forging New Paths Towards Sustainable Development* (Nairobi: UNEP, 2003).

Chapter III

1. D. Nierenberg, "Factory Farming in the Developing World," *World Watch* 16(3) (2003): 10–19.
2. L. R. Brown, *Eco-Economy: Building an Economy for the Earth* (New York: Norton, 2001).
3. Brown, *Eco-Economy: Building an Economy for the Earth;* see also FAO-STAT Food Balance Sheets Database (www.apps.fao.org/page/collections?subset=agriculture) (2003).
4. FAOSTAT Food Balance Sheets Database (www.apps.fao.org/page/collections?subset=agriculture) (2003).
5. Based on M. W. Rosegrant, M. S. Paisner, S. Meijer, and J. Witcover, *2020 Global Food Outlook* (Washington, DC: International Food Policy Research Institute, 2001).
6. FAOSTAT Food Balance Sheets Database (www.apps.fao.org/page/collections?subset=agriculture) (2003).
7. Organization for Economic Cooperation and Development, *Sustainable Consumption: Sector Case Study Series* (Paris, France:OECD, 2001).
8. FAOSTAT Food Balance Sheets Database (www.apps.fao.org/page/collections?subset=agriculture) (2003).
9. Nierenberg, "Factory Farming in the Developing World"; D. Tilman et al., "Forecasting Agriculturally Driven Global Environmental Change," *Science* 292 (2001): 281–284.
10. C. F. Nicholson, R. W. Blake, R. S. Reid, and J. Schelhas, "Environmental Impacts of Livestock in the Developing World," *Technology Review* 43(2) (2001): 7–17.
11. S. Subak, "Global Environmental Costs of Beef Production," *Ecological Economics* 30 (1999): 79–91; Worldwatch Institute, *Vital Signs 2002* (New York: Norton, 2002).
12. L. R. Brown, *Earth Policy Reader 2002* (New York: Norton, 2002); U.S. Environmental Protection Agency, "Ruminant Livestock and the Global Environment" (www.epa.gov/rlep/sustain.htm) (2003).
13. Worldwatch Institute, *Vital Signs 2002.*
14. Nierenberg, "Factory Farming in the Developing World."
15. FAOSTAT Food Balance Sheets Database (www.apps.fao.org/page/collections?subset=agriculture) (2003).

16. Brown, *Earth Policy Reader 2002*.

17. V. Smil, *Feeding the World: A Challenge for the Twenty-First Century* (Cambridge, MA: MIT Press, 2000).

18. FAOSTAT Food Balance Sheets Database (www.apps.fao.org/page/collections?subset=agriculture) (2003).

19. Brown, *Earth Policy Reader 2002*.

20. Brown, *Earth Policy Reader 2002;* U.S. Department of Agriculture, *Production, Supply, and Distribution* (Washington, DC: USDA, 2002); U.S. Department of Agriculture Foreign Agricultural Service, *Grain, World Markets and Trade* (Washington, DC: USDA Foreign Agricultural Service, 2002).

21. L. R. Brown, *World Facing Fourth Consecutive Grain Harvest Shortfall* (Washington, DC: Earth Policy Institute, 2003).

22. Brown, *Earth Policy Reader 2002*.

23. Rosegrant et al., *2020 Global Food Outlook;* Brown, *Earth Policy Reader 2002;* C. Delgado, M. Rosegrant, H. Steinfeld, S. Ehui, and C. Courbois, *Livestock to 2020: The Next Food Revolution* (Washington, DC: International Food Policy Research Institute, 1999); MEDEA Group, *China Agriculture: Cultivated Land Area, Grain Projections, and Implications* (Washington, DC: U.S. National Intelligence Council, 1997).

24. J. Rifkin, *The World's Problems on a Plate: Meat Production is Making the Rich Ill and the Poor Hungry* (Washington, DC: Foundation on Economic Trends, 2002).

25. Food and Agriculture Organization, *The State of Food Insecurity 2002* (www.fao.org/DOCREP/005/Y7352E/Y7352E00.HTM) (2002).

26. FAOSTAT Food Balance Sheets Database (www.apps.fao.org/page/collections?subset=agriculture) (2003).

27. Rifkin, *The World's Problems on a Plate: Meat Production is Making the Rich Ill and the Poor Hungry*.

28. Rosegrant et al., *2020 Global Food Outlook*.

29. S. L. Postel, *Pillars of Sand: Can the Irrigation Miracle Last?* (New York: Norton, 1999).

30. S. L. Postel, "Redesigning Irrigated Agriculture," in L. R. Brown et al., *State of the World 2001* (New York: Norton, 2001).

31. Center for a New American Dream, "Turn the Tide: Nine Actions for the Planet" (www.newdream.org/tttoffline/actions.html) (2003).

32. Postel, "Redesigning Irrigated Agriculture."

33. D. Seckler, D. Molden, and R. Barker, *Water Scarcity in the Twenty-First Century* (Colombo, Sri Lanka: International Water Management Institute, 1998).

34. Postel, *Pillars of Sand: Can the Irrigation Miracle Last?*
35. S. L. Postel, *Last Oasis: Facing Water Scarcity* (New York: Norton, 1997).
36. M. W. Rosegrant, X. Cai, and S. A. Cline, *World Water and Food 2025: Dealing with Scarcity* (Washington, DC: International Food Policy Research Institute, 2002).
37. A. T. Wolfe, *Water, Conflict and Co-operation* (Washington, DC: International Food Policy Research Institute, 2001).
38. S. L. Postel and A. T. Wolf, "Dehydrating Conflict," *Foreign Policy*, September 18, 2001. 2–9; see also P. H. Gleick, A. Singh, and H. Shi, *Threats to the World's Freshwater Resources* (Oakland, CA: Pacific Institute for Studies in Development, Environment, and Security, 2001).
39. Postel, "Redesigning Irrigated Agriculture."
40. N. Myers and J. Kent, *Perverse Subsidies: How Tax Dollars Can Undercut the Environment and the Economy* (Washington, DC: Island Press, 2001).
41. Postel, "Redesigning Irrigated Agriculture"; P. H. Gleick, *The World's Water 2000–2001* (Washington, DC: Island Press, 2000); T. Gardner-Outlaw and R. Engelman, *Sustaining Water, Easing Scarcity: A Second Update* (Washington, DC: Population Action International, 1997).
42. Myers and Kent, *Perverse Subsidies: How Tax Dollars Can Undercut the Environment and the Economy.*
43. D. Pimentel, O. Bailey, P. Kim, E. Mullaney, J. Calabrese, L. Walman, F. Nelson, and X. Yao, "Will Limits of the Earth's Resources Control Human Numbers?" *Environment, Development and Sustainability* 1(1) (1999): 19–39.
44. Rosegrant et al., *2020 Global Food Outlook;* see also Delgado et al., *Livestock to 2020: The Next Food Revolution.*
45. Brown, *Eco-Economy: Building an Economy for the Earth.*
46. D. Tilford, "Biodiversity to Go: The Hidden Costs of Beef Consumption" (www.newdream.org/food/beefcost.html) (2002).
47. G. Gardner and B. Halweil, "Nourishing the Underfed and Overfed," in L. R. Brown et al., *State of the World 2000* (New York: Norton, 2000), 59–78; J. O. Hill et al., "Obesity and the Environment: Where Do We Go From Here?" *Science* 299 (2003): 853–855.
48. Gardner and Halweil, "Nourishing the Underfed and Overfed."
49. Brown, *Eco-Economy: Building an Economy for the Earth.*
50. Gardner and Halweil, "Nourishing the Underfed and Overfed"; E. Schlosser, *Fast Food Nation: What the All-American Meal is Doing to the World* (New York: Allen Lane/The Penguin Press, 2001); G. Critser, *Fat Land: How Americans Became the Fattest People in the World* (London: Allen Lane, 2003).

51. Schlosser, *Fast Food Nation: What the All-American Meal is Doing to the World.*

52. World Health Organization, *Heart Attack Deaths on the Rise* (Geneva: WHO, 2002).

53. World Health Organization, *Heart Attack Deaths on the Rise.*

54. Brown, *Earth Policy Reader 2002.*

55. R. Goodland and D. Pimentel, eds., *Ecological Integrity: Integrating Environment, Conservation, and Health* (Washington, DC: Island Press, 2001).

56. Schlosser, *Fast Food Nation: What the All-American Meal is Doing to the World.*

57. Nestle, *Food Politics: How the Food Industry Influences Nutrition and Health* (Berkeley: University of California Press, 2002).

Chapter IV

1. M. Brower and W. Leon, "U.S. Consumption and the Environment," in A. R. Chapman, R. L. Petersen, and B. Smith-Moran, eds., *Consumption, Population, and Sustainability* (Washington, DC: Island Press, 2000), 97–107.

2. Energy Information Administration, *International Energy Outlook 2003* (Washington DC: U.S. Department of Energy, 2003); see also International Energy Agency, *Key World Energy Statistics* (Paris: IEA, 2002).

3. World Resources Institute Earthtrends Database on CO_2 Emissions (www.earthtrends.wri.org) (2003).

4. O. Dzioubinski and R. Chapman, *Trends in Consumption and Production: Selected Minerals and Consumption* (New York: United Nations, 1999).

5. Energy Information Administration International Energy Database (www.eia.doe.gov/emeu/international/contents.html) (2003).

6. Dzioubinski and Chapman, *Trends in Consumption and Production: Selected Minerals and Consumption;* United Nations Economic and Social Commission for Asia and the Pacific, *Guidebook on Promotion of Sustainable Energy Consumption: Consumer Organizations and Efficient Energy Use in the Residential Sector* (Bangkok: United Nations Economic and Social Commission for Asia and the Pacific, 2002).

7. Asian Demographics Limited, *Projected Growth of Household Consumption of Electricity in China to 2011* (www.asiandemographics.com) (2002).

8. International Energy Agency, *Cool Appliances: Policy Strategies for Energy-Efficient Homes* (Paris: IEA, 2003); United Nations Economic and Social Commission for Asia and the Pacific, *Guidebook on Promotion of Sustainable Energy Consumption: Consumer Organizations and Efficient Energy Use in the Residential Sector.*

9. J. H. Spangenberg and S. Lorek, "Environmentally Sustainable Household Consumption: From Aggregate Environmental Pressures to Priority Fields of Action," *Ecological Economics* 43 (2002): 127–140; Organization for Economic Cooperation and Development, *Towards More Sustainable Household Consumption Patterns: Indicators to Measure Progress* (Paris: OECD, 1998).

10. J. Thorne and M. Svozzo, *Leaking Electricity: Standby and Off-Mode Power Consumption in Consumer Electronics and Household Appliances* (Washington, DC: American Council for an Energy-Efficient Economy, 1998); see also International Energy Agency, "Things That Go Blip in the Night: Standby Power and How to Limit It," *@tmosphere* July 6, 2001: 26; B. Lebot, A. Meier and A. Anglade, *Global Implications of Standby Power Use* (http://eetd.lbl.gov/EA/Reports/46019.pdf) (2000).

11. R. Heede, *Cool Citizens: Household Solutions* (Snowmass, CO: Rocky Mountain Institute, 2002); International Energy Agency, "Things That Go Blip in the Night: Standby Power and How to Limit It."

12. Dzioubinski and Chapman, *Trends in Consumption and Production: Selected Minerals and Consumption;* Spangenberg and Lorek, "Environmentally Sustainable Household Consumption: From Aggregate Environmental Pressures to Priority Fields of Action."

13. P. Hawken, A. B. Lovins, and L. H. Lovins, *Natural Capitalism* (Boston: Little, Brown, 1999); Heede, *Cool Citizens: Household Solutions.*

14. Heede, *Cool Citizens: Household Solutions.*

15. C. Flavin, "America's Energy Problem," *World Watch* 14(4) (2001): 11; Hawken et al., *Natural Capitalism.*

16. J. Romm, A. Rosenfeld, and S. Hermann, The Internet Economy and Global Warming (www.cool-companies.org/energy/paper1.cfm) (1999).

17. J. L. Sawin, "Wind Power's Rapid Growth Continues," in Worldwatch Institute, *Vital Signs 2003* (New York: Norton, 2003), 38–39.

18. C. Flavin, "Wind Energy Growth Continues," in *Vital Signs 2001* (New York: Norton, 2001), 44–45.

19. Flavin, "America's Energy Problem."

20. B. Fischlowitz-Roberts, *Sales of Solar Cells Take Off* (Washington, DC: Earth Policy Institute, 2002); H. Scheer, *Renewable Energy for a Sustainable Global Future* (London: Earthscan, 2002).

21. J. Makower and R. Pernick, *Clean Tech: Profits and Potential* (Oakland, CA: Clean Edge, 2001); see also M. I. Hoffert et al., "Advanced Technology Paths to Global Climate Stability: Energy for a Greenhouse

Planet," *Science* 298 (2002): 981–987; D. Pimentel et al., "Renewable Energy: Current and Potential Issues," *BioScience* 52 (2002): 1111–1120.

22. Energy Information Administration International Energy Database; see also S. Dunn, "Carbon Emissions Continue to Decline," in Worldwatch Institute, *Vital Signs 2001* (New York: Norton, 2001).

23. C. Xiaozhu, *Policies and Efforts to Reduce Standby Power Energy Consumption in China* (Beijing: Science and Technology Department, Ministry of Information Industry, 2001).

24. United Nations Environment Programme, *Forging New Paths Towards Sustainable Development* (Nairobi: UNEP, 2003).

25. A. B. Lovins, *U.S. Energy Security Linked to Efficiency* (Snowmass, CO: Rocky Mountain Institute, 2003).

26. M. Scholand, "Compact Fluorescents Set Record," in Worldwatch Institute, *Vital Signs 2002* (New York: Norton, 2002).

27. K. C. Gupta, *Energy and Environment in India: A Study of Energy Management* (New Delhi: Gyam Publishing, 2002); R. N. Hattacharya and S. Poul, "Sectoral Changes in Consumption and Intensity of Energy in India," *Indian Economic Review* 36 (2001): 381–392; R. K. Pachauri and J. Spreng, "Direct and Indirect Energy Requirements of Households in India," *Energy Policy* 30 (2002): 511–523.

28. Hawken et al., *Natural Capitalism*.

29. M. Wackernagel et al., "Tracking the Ecological Overshoot of the Human Economy," *Proceedings of National Academy of Sciences* (USA) 99 (2002): 9266–9271; see also N. Chambers, C. Simmons, and M. Wackernagel, *Sharing Nature's Interest: Ecological Footprints as an Indicator of Sustainability* (London: Earthscan, 2001); J. Lo, ed., *WWF Living Planet Report 2002* (Gland, Switzerland: World Wide Fund for Nature, 2002).

30. W. Rees, "Revisiting Carrying Capacity: Area-Based Indicators of Sustainability," *Population and Environment* 17(2) (1996): 9.

31. M. Wackernagel et al., "Tracking the Ecological Overshoot of the Human Economy."

32. N. Chambers et al., *Sharing Nature's Interest: Ecological Footprints as an Indicator of Sustainability*.

33. O. A. Dodds, *The City Limits* (London: Best Foot Forward Consultancy Limited, 2002).

34. T. Dietz and E. A. Rosa, "Effects of Population and Affluence on CO_2 Emissions," *Proceedings of the National Academy of Sciences of the USA* 94 (1997): 175–179.

35. World Resources Institute, *World Resources 2000–2001* (Washington, DC: World Resources Institute, 2000).

36. P. R. Ehrlich and J. P. Holdren, "Impact of Population Growth," *Science* 171 (1971): 1212–1217.

37. J. P. Holdren, "Environmental Degradation: Population, Affluence, Technology, and Sociopolitical Factors," *Environment* 42(6) (2000): 4–5.

38. T. Princen, M. Maniates, and K. Conca, eds., *Confronting Consumption* (Cambridge, MA: MIT Press, 2002).

39. For discussion of this theme, see Dietz and Rosa, "Effects of Population and Affluence on CO_2 Emissions."

40. Population Reference Bureau, *World Population Data Sheet 2003* (Washington, DC: Population Reference Bureau, 2003); United Nations Population Division, *World Population Prospects: The 2000 Revision* (New York: United Nations, 2001).

41. United Nations Population Division, *World Population Prospects: The 2002 Revision.*

42. United Nations Population Division, *World Population Prospects: The 2002 Revision.*

43. A. de Sherbinin, *Population and Consumption Issues for Environmentalists* (Washington DC: Population Reference Bureau, 1993); P. R. Ehrlich and A. H. Ehrlich, *Betrayal of Science and Reason: How Anti-Environmental Rhetoric Threatens Our Future* (Washington DC: Island Press, 1996); N. Myers, "Consumption in Relation to Population, Environment and Development," *The Environmentalist* 17 (1997): 33–44; D. Pimentel, O. Bailey, P. Kim, E. Mullaney, J. Calabrese, L. Walman, F. Nelson, and X. Yao, "Will Limits of the Earth's Resources Control Human Numbers?" *Environment, Development and Sustainability* 1(1) (1999): 19–39.

44. United Nations Population Division, *World Population Prospects: The 2002 Revision.*

45. A. Sen, "Many Faces of Gender Inequality," *The Frontline* (India), October 27–November 9, 2001, http://www.hinduonnet.com/fline/fl1822/18220040.htm.

Chapter V

1. World Bank, *World Development Indicators 2003* (www.worldbank.org/data/wdi2003/); see also Asian Development Bank, *Asian Development Outlook 2000* (Manila: Asian Development Bank, 2000); J. Becker, *The Chinese* (London: John Murray, 2000); M. D. Swaine and A. J. Tellis,

Interpreting China's Grand Strategy: Past, Present, and Future (Santa Monica, CA: RAND Center for Asia-Pacific Policy, 2000).

2. G. C. Chow, *China's Economic Transformation* (Oxford, UK: Blackwells, 2002); C. H. Kwan, *China in Transition* (www.rieti.go.jp/en/china/archive.html); China Statistics Press, *China Statistical Year Book 2001* (Beijing: China Statistics Press, 2001); M. Pei, "China's Split Personality," in *The Five Faces of China*, World Economic Forum special issue of *Newsweek*, Fall/Winter 2002: 6–13; see also M. Pei, "Will China Become Another Indonesia?" *Foreign Policy* (Fall 1999): 12–18.

3. FAOSTAT Food Balance Sheets Database 2003 (www.apps.fao.org/page/collections?subset=agriculture); Far Eastern Economic Review, "World's Manufacturing Center: China," *Far Eastern Economic Review*, October 17, 2002 (www.feer.com).

4. D. Ben-Ami, *Cowardly Capitalism: The Myth of the Global Financial Casino* (New York: John Wiley, 2001); see also International Finance Corporation, *China's Emerging Private Enterprise: Prospects for the New Century* (Washington, DC: International Finance Corporation, 2000).

5. World Bank, *World Development Indicators 2003* (www.worldbank.org/data/wdi2003/).

6. World Bank, *World Development Indicators 2003* (www.worldbank.org/data/wdi2003/).

7. Becker, *The Chinese;* Chow, *China's Economic Transformation;* C.H. Kwan, *China in Transition;* China Statistics Press, *China Statistical Year Book 2001;* N. R. Lardy, *Integrating China into the Global Economy* (Washington, DC: Brookings Institution Press, 2001); N. Myers and J. Kent, "New Consumers: The Influence of Affluence on the Environment," *Proceedings of the National Academy of Sciences* (USA) 100 (2003): 4963–4968.

8. D. S. Davis, "A Revolution in Consumption," in D. S. Davis, ed., *The Consumer Revolution in Urban China* (Berkeley: University of California Press, 2000), 1–22; M. Feliciano, "China's Newly-Rich Incomes Close to NIE Levels" (Taiwan: News 2003 [article discontinued online]); Kwan, *China in Transition;* China Statistics Press, *China Statistical Year Book 2001;* J. Leow, *Fears Grow Over China's Widening Rich-Poor Divide* (Singapore: Singapore Press Holdings, 2003).

9. Kwan, *China in Transition;* China Statistics Press, *China Statistical Year Book 2001.*

10. Chow, *China's Economic Transformation.*

11. Davis, "A Revolution in Consumption"; Feliciano, *China's Newly-Rich*

Incomes Close to NIE Levels; Kwan, *China in Transition;* China Statistics Press, *China Statistical Year Book 2001;* Leow, *Fears Grow Over China's Widening Rich-Poor Divide.*

12. Kwan, *China in Transition;* China Statistics Press, *China Statistical Year Book 2001;* Pei, "China's Split Personality."

13. Chow, *China's Economic Transformation;* Kwan, *China in Transition;* China Statistics Press, *China Statistical Year Book 2001;* Pei, "China's Split Personality."

14. Davis, "A Revolution in Consumption"; G. Ruoqun, "Forecast of China's Home Electric Appliance Market Trend" (www.chinaproducts. com/eng2/content/contf56.php) (2001).

15. Asian Demographics Limited, *Projected Growth of Household Consumption of Electricity in China to 2011* (www.asiandemographics.com) (2002); Freedonia Group, Inc., *World Major Household Appliances* (Cleveland, OH: The Freedonia Group, 2002); Ruoqun, "Forecast of China's Home Electric Appliance Market Trend."

16. D. Hale and L. H. Hale, "China Takes Off," *Foreign Affairs* 82(6) (2003): 36–53; Kwan, *China in Transition;* China Statistics Press, *China Statistical Year Book 2001;* Pei, "China's Split Personality"; R. Terrill, *The New Chinese Empire: What It Means for the United States* (New York: Basic Books, 2003)

17. Hale and Hale, "China Takes Off"; World Bank, *World Development Indicators 2003* (www.worldbank.org/data/wdi2003/).

18. World Bank, *World Development Indicators 2003* (www.worldbank.org/data/wdi2003/); see also M. Branko, *Income, Inequality, and Poverty During the Transition from Planned to Market Economy* (Washington, DC: The World Bank, 1998); Conghua Li and Deloitte and Touche Consulting Group, *China: The Consumer Revolution* (Singapore: John Wiley & Sons [Asia] Pte. Ltd., 1998); F. Itoh, ed., *China in the Twenty-First Century: Politics, Economy, and Society* (Tokyo: United Nations University Press, 1997); Swaine and Tellis, *Interpreting China's Grand Strategy: Past, Present, and Future.*

19. Chow, *China's Economic Transformation;* L. Su-Chen and X. Yu-Qing, *China's Sustainable Development Framework* (Tokyo: United Nations University Press, 1999); B. Murray, *China's Prospects* (Beijing: Asian Development Bank, 2002); Far Eastern Economic Review, "World's Manufacturing Center: China"; A. Zhang, *Hidden Dragon: Unleashing China's Private Sector* (London: China Business Centre, 2003).

20. Chow, *China's Economic Transformation;* Kwan, *China in Transition;* China

Statistics Press, *China Statistical Year Book 2001;* Pei, "China's Split Personality."

21. W. Lutz and A. Goujon, *The World's Changing Human Capital Stock* (Laxemburg, Austria: International Institute for Applied Systems Analysis, 2001); World Business Council for Sustainable Development, *Trends to Watch in China* (Geneva: World Business Council for Sustainable Development, 2002).

22. Davis, "A Revolution in Consumption"; Myers and Kent, "New Consumers: The Influence of Affluence on the Environment"; K. G. Nealer, China's Middle Class (www.usda.gov/oce/waob/oc2002/speeches/nealerppt.pdf) (2002); J. Studwell, *The China Dream: The Elusive Quest for the Greatest Untapped Market on Earth* (London: Profile Books, 2002).

23. FAOSTAT Food Balance Sheets Database 2003 (www.apps.fao.org/page/collections?subset=agriculture); see also L. R. Brown, *Eco-Economy: Building an Economy for the Earth* (New York: Norton, 2001); S. Fan and M. J. Cohen, *Critical Choices for China's Agricultural Policy* (Washington, DC: International Food Policy Research Institute, 1999).

24. M. W. Rosegrant, M. S. Paisner, S. Meijer, and J. Witcover, *2020 Global Food Outlook* (Washington, DC: International Food Policy Research Institute, 2001); see also C. Delgado, M. Rosegrant, H. Steinfeld, S. Ehui, and C. Courbois, *Livestock to 2020: The Next Food Revolution* (Washington, DC: International Food Policy Research Institute, 2001); P. Pinstrup-Andersen, R. Pandya-Lorch, and M. W. Rosegrant, *World Food Prospects: Crucial Issues for the Early Twenty-First Century* (Washington, DC: International Food Policy Research Institute, 1999).

25. Food and Agriculture Organization, *Livestock Production Yearbook* (Rome: Food and Agriculture Organization, 2002).

26. M. Shah and M. Strong, *Food in the Twenty-First Century: From Science to Sustainable Agriculture* (Washington, DC: CGIAR and World Bank, 1999).

27. L. R. Brown and C. Flavin, "China's Challenge to the United States and to the Earth," *World Watch* 8(5) (1996); K. E. Calder, *Asia's Deadly Triangle: How Arms, Energy and Growth Threaten to Destabilize Asia-Pacific* (London: Nicholas Brealey, 1996).

28. Brown, *Eco-Economy: Building an Economy for the Earth.*

29. G. K. Heilig, *Can China Feed Itself? A System for Evaluation of Policy Options* (Laxemburg, Austria: International Institute for Applied Systems Analysis, 1999).

30. L. R. Brown, "Eco-Economy Update: World Facing Fourth Consecutive

Grain Harvest Shortfall" (www.earth-policy.org/Updates/Update28. htm) (2003).

31. L. R. Brown et al., *State of the World 1998* (New York: Norton, 1998); Heilig, *Can China Feed Itself? A System for Evaluation of Policy Options;* G. Pauli, *Upsizing: The Road to Zero Emissions, More Jobs, More Income and No Pollution* (Sheffield, UK: Greenleaf Publishing, 1998).

32. Brown, *Eco-Economy: Building an Economy for the Earth.*

33. FAOSTAT Food Balance Sheets Database 2003 (www.apps.fao.org/ page/collections?subset=agriculture); see also Jian Song, *No Impasse for China's Development* (Beijing: State Science and Technology Commission, 1997).

34. Delgado et al., *Livestock to 2020: The Next Food Revolution;* World Bank, *China: 2020* (New York: Oxford University Press, 1997); see also Rosegrant et al/, *2020 Global Food Outlook.*

35. L. R. Brown, *Who Will Feed China? Wakeup Call for a Small Planet* (New York: Norton, 1995); Delgado et al., *Livestock to 2020: The Next Food Revolution;* Heilig, "Can China Feed Itself? A System for Evaluation of Policy Options"; MEDEA Group, *China Agriculture: Cultivated Land Area, Grain Projections, and Implications* (Washington, DC: U.S. National Intelligence Council, 1997); Rosegrant et al., *2020 Global Food Outlook.*

36. Brown, *Eco-Economy: Building an Economy for the Earth;* He Qingcheng, *The North China Plain and its Aquifers* (Beijing: Geological Environmental Monitoring Institute, 2001); World Bank, *China: Agenda for Water Sector Strategy for North China* (Washington, DC: The World Bank, 2001).

37. Brown, *Eco-Economy: Building an Economy for the Earth;* FAOSTAT 2003 (www.fao.org).

38. L. R. Brown, "Worsening Water Shortages Threaten China's Food Security" (www.earth-policy.org/Updates/Update1.htm) (2001).

39. FAOSTAT Food Balance Sheets Database 2003 (www.apps.fao.org/ page/collections?subset=agriculture).

40. K. Riley, "Motor Vehicles in China: The Impact of Demographic and Economic Changes," *Population and Environment* 23 (2002): 479–494; C. T. Whipple, "China Holds Promise for Automakers," *International Herald Tribune*, October 20, 2001.

41. D. Murphy, "Car Making: A Consumer-Driven Market," *Far Eastern Economic Review*, February 22, 2001 (www.feer.com); World Business Council for Sustainable Development, *Trends to Watch in China.*

42. World Bank, *World Development Indicators 2003* (www.worldbank.org/ data/wdi2003/).

43. China Internet Information Center, *More Chinese Plan to Buy Private Cars This Year* (Beijing: China Internet Information Center, 2002); see also State Statistic Bureau of China, *Car Numbers in 2000* (Beijing: State Statistic Bureau of China, 2000).

44. Hale and Hale, "China Takes Off"; J. Madslien, "China Car Sector Seeks World Dominance," *BBC News*, June 7, 2002 (http://news.bbc.co.uk/2/hi/business/2026707.stm).

45. Riley, "Motor Vehicles in China: The Impact of Demographic and Economic Changes"; Murphy, "Car Making: A Consumer-Driven Market"; see also K. A. Baumert and N. Kete, *World Developing Countries' Carbon Emissions Swamp Global Emissions Reduction Efforts?* (Washington, DC: World Resources Institute, 2002); L. Schipper, C. Marie-Lilliu, and G. Lewis-Davis, *Rapid Motorization in the Largest Countries in Asia: Implications for Oil, Carbon Dioxide and Transportation* (Paris: International Energy Agency, 1999).

46. International Trade Association, *China's Automotive Market* (Washington, DC: International Trade Association, U.S. Department of Commerce, 2002); Whipple, "China Holds Promise for Automakers."

47. Murphy, "Car Making: A Consumer-Driven Market"; *People's Daily Online*, (http://english.peopledaily.com.cn) (2001).

48. O. August, "Oliver August in Beijing," *London Times*, April 22, 2002.

49. Brown, *Eco-Economy: Building an Economy for the Earth;* see also International Energy Agency, *World Energy Outlook 2002* (Paris: IEA, 2002); Energy Information Administration, *China* (Washington, DC: U.S. Department of Energy, 2001).

50. Brown, *Eco-Economy: Building an Economy for the Earth;* D. Guangwei and L. Shishun, "Analysis of Impetuses to Change of Agricultural Land Resources in China," *Bulletin of the Chinese Academy of Sciences* 13(1) (1999) (www.bulletin.ac.cn/issues/99-1/10.htm).

51. Energy Information Administration, *International Energy Outlook 2001* (Washington DC: U.S. Department of Energy, 2001); Riley, "Motor Vehicles in China: The Impact of Demographic and Economic Changes"; R. Weisbrod, "Solving China's Urban Crisis: China's Transportation Energy Future," *Journal of Urban Technology* 6 (1999): 89100.

52. M. H. Chang, *The Labors of Sisyphus: The Economic Development of Communist China* (New Brunswick, NJ: Transaction Books, 1997).

53. Ibid.

54. D. Sperling and H. Zhou, *Limiting Greenhouse Gases in India and China*

(Davis, CA: Institute of Transportation Studies, University of California, 2002).

55. Ruoqun, "Forecast of China's Home Electric Appliance Market Trend."

56. China's State Statistical Bureau, *Indicators of Energy Use* (Beijing: China's State Statistical Bureau, 2001).

57. Asian Demographics Limited, *Projected Growth of Household Consumption of Electricity in China to 2011;* Hale and Hale, "China Takes Off."

58. A. Baumert, R. Bhandari, and N. Kete, *What Might a Developing Country Climate Commitment Look Like?* (Washington DC: World Resources Institute, 1999); N. Myers and J. Kent, *Perverse Subsidies: How Tax Dollars Can Undercut the Environment and the Economy* (Washington, DC: Island Press, 2001); World Bank, *Expanding the Measure of Wealth: Indicators of Environmentally Sustainable Development* (Washington, DC: The World Bank, 1997).

59. Energy Information Administration International Energy Database; World Bank, *World Development Indicators 2003* (www.worldbank.org/data/wdi2003/).

60. D. G. Streets et al., "Recent Reductions in China's Greenhouse Gas Emissions," *Science* 294 (2002): 1835–1837; Energy Information Administration International Energy Database.

61. J. Byrne, B. Shen, and X. Li, "The Challenge of Sustainability: Balancing China's Energy, Economic and Environmental Goals," *Energy Policy* 24 (1996): 455–462.

62. BP/Amoco, *Statistical Review of World Energy 2003* (Surrey, UK: BP/AMOCO, 2003); see also S. Dunn, "King Coal's Weakening Grip on Power," *World Watch* 12(5) (2001): 10–19; Energy Information Administration International Energy Database.

63. BP/Amoco, *Statistical Review of World Energy;* see also E. D. Larson et al., "Future Implications of China's Energy-Technology Choices," *Energy Policy* 31 (2003): 1189–1204.

64. Energy Information Administration, *International Energy Outlook 2003* (Washington, DC: U.S. Department of Energy, 2003); see also B. A. Finamore and T. M. Szymanski, "Taming the Dragon Heads: Controlling Air Emissions from Power Plants in China—An Analysis of China's Air Pollution Policy and Regulatory Framework," *Environmental Law Institute* 32 (2002): 11,439-11,458.

65. Energy Information Administration, *International Energy Outlook 2002* (Washington, DC: U.S. Department of Energy, 2002).

66. Energy Information Administration, *International Energy Outlook 2002.*

67. Brown, *Eco-Economy: Building an Economy for the Earth*.
68. C. Flavin and S. Dunn, "Reinventing the Energy System," in L. R. Brown et al., *State of the World 1999* (New York: Norton, 1999), 22–40.
69. O. Dzioubinski and R. Chipman, *Trends in Consumption and Production: Household Energy Consumption* (New York: Department of Economic and Social Affairs, 1999); Ruoqun, "Forecast of China's Home Electric Appliance Market Trend"; J. Sinton et al., *Status Report on Energy Efficiency Policy and Programs in China* (Berkeley, CA: Lawrence Berkeley National Laboratory, 1999).
70. World Health Organization, *Health and Environment in Sustainable Development: Five Years After the Earth Summit* (Geneva: WHO, 1997).
71. World Bank, *World Development Indicators 2003* (www.worldbank.org/ data/wdi2003/); M. Farley, "The Grittiest Air on Earth: Costs from Pollution Stunt Growth," *Population Press* 5(5) (1999): 9–10; United Nations Development Programme, *Human Development Report 1998* (New York: Oxford University Press, 1998).
72. M. H. Chang, "China's Ecological Nightmare," *Focus* 9(1) (1999): 36 (published by the Carrying Capacity Network).
73. J. Byrne, B. Shen, and W. Wallace, "The Economics of Sustainable Energy for Rural Development: A Study of Renewable Energy in Rural China," *Energy Policy* 26(1) (1996): 45–54; see also W. Chandler, Zhou Dadi, J. Logan, Guo Yuan, and Shi Yingyi, *China's Electric Power Options: An Analysis of Economic and Environmental Costs* (Washington, DC: Pacific Northwest National Laboratory, 1998).
74. Editing Board of China Environmental Yearbook, *China Environmental Yearbook* (Beijing: EBCEY , 1997); World Bank, *Clear Water, Blue Skies: China's Environment in the New Century* (Washington, DC: The World Bank, 1997).
75. V. Smil and M. Yushi, *The Economic Costs of China's Environmental Degradation* (Cambridge, MA: American Academy of Arts and Sciences, 1998); see also A. Frank, "Solving China's Environmental Problems: Policy Options," *Environment and Security Report* (Washington, DC: Woodrow Wilson Center, 1998): 68-70.
76. L. R. Brown, *Paving the Planet: Cars and Crops Competing for Land* (Washington, DC: Worldwatch Institute, 2001).
77. Brown, *Eco-Economy: Building an Economy for the Earth*.
78. Ibid.
79. Ibid.; He Qingcheng, *The North China Plain and its Aquifers*.
80. Brown, *Eco-Economy: Building an Economy for the Earth*; S. L. Postel,

"Redesigning Irrigated Agriculture," in L. R. Brown et al., *State of the World 2000* (New York: Norton, 2000); L. Yonggong and J. B. Penson, *China's Sustainable Agriculture and Regional Implications* (College Station, TX: Department of Agricultural Economics, Texas A & M University, 1997).

81. Brown, *Eco-Economy: Building an Economy for the Earth.*
82. World Bank, *China: Agenda for Water Sector Strategy for North China;* see also MEDEA Group, *China Agriculture: Cultivated Land Area, Grain Projections, and Implications;* A. Nyberg and S. Rozelle, *Accelerating China's Rural Transformation* (Washington, DC: The World Bank, 1999); R. Wang, "China Water Vision in the First Quarter of the 21st Century," in L. Fu-Chen, H. Tokuda, and N. S. Cooray, eds., *The Sustainable Future of the Global System III* (Tokyo: Institute of Advanced Studies, United Nations University, 2000), 241–254.
83. L. R. Brown and B. Halweil, "China's Water Shortage Could Shake World Food Security," *World Watch* 11(4) (1998): 10–21; Yonggong and Penson, *China's Sustainable Agriculture and Regional Implications.*
84. World Bank, *China Air, Land and Water: Environmental Priorities for a New Millennium* (Washington, DC: The World Bank, 2001).
85. T. Akita and Y. Nakanura, *Green GDP Estimates in China, Indonesia, and Japan* (Tokyo: United Nations University, 2000); Chang, "China's Ecological Nightmare"; A. Frank, "Solving China's Environmental Problems: Policy Options"; F. Lo, *A Sustainable Development Framework for Developing Countries: The Case of China* (Tokyo: Institute of Advanced Studies, United Nations University, 1998); T. Palanivel, *Sustainable Development of China, India and Indonesia: Trends and Responses* (Tokyo: Institute of Advanced Studies, United Nations University, 2001); Smil and Yushi, *The Economic Costs of China's Environmental Degradation.*
86. Brown, *Eco-Economy: Building an Economy for the Earth.*
87. United Nations Population Division, *World Population Prospects: The 2002 Revision* (New York: United Nations Population Division, 2003).
88. Brown, *Eco-Economy: Building an Economy for the Earth.*
89. Brown, *Eco-Economy: Building an Economy for the Earth;* M. Hertsgaard, "Our Real China Problem," *Atlantic Monthly,* November 1997, 97–114; V. Smil, "China Shoulders the Cost of Environmental Change," *Environment* 39(6) (1997): 6–9, 33–37.
90. Brown, *Eco-Economy: Building an Economy for the Earth.*
91. Based on United Nations Population Division, *World Population Prospects: The 2002 Revision* and World Bank, *World Development Indicators 2003* (www.worldbank.org/data/wdi2003/).

92. M. Gurtov, *Pacific Asia? Prospects for Security and Cooperation in East Asia* (Lanham, MA: Rowman and Littlefield, 2002); J. Mearsheimer, *The Tragedy of Great Power Politics* (New York: Norton, 2001).

Chapter VI

1. S. Cohen, *India: Emerging Power* (Washington, DC: Brookings Institution Press, 2001); G. Das, *India Unbound: A Personal Account of a Social and Economic Revolution from Independence to the Global Information Age* (New York: Knopf, 2001); T. Dyson, R. Cassen, and L. Visari, *21st Century India: Population, Economy, Human Development and Environment* (Oxford: Oxford University Press, in press); Y. Huang and T. Khanna, "Can India Overtake China?" *Foreign Policy* July/August (2003): 74–81; A. Parthasarathi, "A Champion of New Technologies," *Nature* 422 (2003): 17–18.

2. K. Bradsher, "India Slips Far Behind China, Once Its Close Economic Rival," *New York Times*, November 29, 2002; Far Eastern Economic Review, "World's Manufacturing Center: China," *Far Eastern Economic Review* (October 17, 2002) (www.feer.com); B. Murray, *China's Prospects* (Beijing: Asian Development Bank, 2002); J. Srinivasan, "Playing Catch-Up with China," *Hindu Business Line* 9(133) (2002): 1–8.

3. B. Groombridge and M. D. Jenkins, *Global Biodiversity: Earth's Living Resources in the 21st Century* (Nairobi and Cambridge, UK: UNEP–World Conservation Monitoring Centre, 2000).

4. L. Fernandes, "Restructuring the New Middle Class in Liberalizing India," *Comparative Studies of South Asia, Africa and the Middle East* 20 (2000): 88–112; P. Varma, *The Great Indian Middle Class* (New Delhi: Viking, 1998).

5. Y. K. Alagh, *India's Sustainable Development Framework: 2020* (Tokyo: Institute for Advanced Studies, United Nations University, 2001); D. Biers, "In India, a Bit of California," *Far Eastern Economic Review*, November 2, 2000 (www.feer.com); Das, *India Unbound: A Personal Account of a Social and Economic Revolution from Independence to the Global Information Age;* N. D. Kristof and S. WuDunn, *Thunder from the East: Portrait of a Rising Asia* (New York: Knopf, 2000).

6. World Bank, *World Development Indicators 2003* (www.worldbank.org/data/wdi2003/).

7. Notably, Asian Development Bank, *Asian Development Outlook 2000* (Manila: Asian Development Bank, 2000); Consumers International Regional Office for Asia and the Pacific, *A Discerning Middle Class? A Preliminary Enquiry of Sustainable Consumption Trends in Selected Countries in the Asia Pacific Region* (Penang, Malaysia: Consumers International

Regional Office for Asia and the Pacific [CI-ROAP], 1998); Das, *India Unbound: A Personal Account of a Social and Economic Revolution from Independence to the Global Information Age;* Alagh, *India's Sustainable Development Framework: 2020;* T. Palanivel, *Implementation of Agenda 21 in Developing Countries* (Tokyo: Institute for Advanced Studies, United Nations University, 2002).

8. National Council for Applied Economics Research, *India Market Demographics Report 2002* (New Delhi: NCAER, 2002) and *Market Information Survey of Households* (New Delhi: NCAER, 2003).

9. N. Myers and J. Kent, "New Consumers: The Influence of Affluence on the Environment," *Proceedings of the National Academy of Sciences* (USA) 100 (2003): 4963–4968.

10. J. Parikh, M. Panda, and N. S. Murthy, *Consumption Pattern Differences and Environmental Implications: A Case Study of India* (Bombay: Indira Gandhi Institute of Development Research, 1994).

11. Authors' calculations, based on Consumers International Regional Office for Asia and the Pacific, *A Discerning Middle Class? A Preliminary Enquiry of Sustainable Consumption Trends in Selected Countries in the Asia Pacific Region* and Myer's visit to India in March 2003.

12. P. Audiret, ed., *India's Energy* (New Delhi: Manobar Publishers, 2000); Tata Energy Research Institute, *Defining an Integrated Energy Strategy for India* (New Delhi: TERI, 2002).

13. Global Insight, *World Overview December 2002* (www.globalinsight.com) (2002); International Monetary Fund, World Economic Outlook Database, April 2003 (www.imf.org/external/pubs/ft/weo/2003/01/data/index.htm); A. P. J. A. Kalam and Y. S. Rajan, *India 2020: A Vision for the New Millennium* (New York: Penguin Books, 1998); Kristof and WuDunn, *Thunder from the East: Portrait of a Rising Asia;* World Bank, *Asia's Development Outlook* (Washington, DC: The World Bank, 2000).

14. World Bank, *World Development Report 1994* (Washington, DC: The World Bank, 1994); World Bank, *World Development Indicators 2003* (www.worldbank.org/data/wdi2003/); see also Das, *India Unbound: A Personal Account of a Social and Economic Revolution from Independence to the Global Information Age.*

15. Calculated by the authors from World Bank, *World Development Indicators 2003* (www.worldbank.org/data/wdi2003/).

16. National Council for Applied Economic Research, *Study of Changes in Consumption Patterns in Rural and Urban Areas: Indian Market Demographics Report, 1998* (New Delhi: NCAER, 1998).

17. Fernandes, "Restructuring the New Middle Class in Liberalizing India"; J. James, *Can Appropriate Products (and Technologies) Capture Mass Markets in Developing Countries? A Case Study from India* (Tilburg, Netherlands: Centre for Economic Research, Tilburg University, 1999); R. Robison and D. Goodman, eds., *The New Rich in Asia: Mobile Phones, McDonalds and Middle-Class Revolution* (New York: Routledge, 1996).

18. United Nations Development Programme, *Human Development Report 2002* (New York: Oxford University Press, 2002); see also World Bank, *World Development Report 1994.*

19. J. E. Garten, *The Big Ten: The Big Emerging Markets and How They Will Change Our Lives* (New York: Basic Books, 1997); J. Naisbitt, *Megatrends Asia: The Eight Asian Megatrends That Are Changing the World* (London: Nicholas Brealey, 1995).

20. World Bank, *World Development Indicators 2003* (www.worldbank.org/data/wdi2003/).

21. P. Pinstrup-Andersen, R. Pandya-Lorch, and M. W. Rosegrant, *World Food Prospects: Crucial Issues for the Early Twenty-First Century* (Washington, DC: International Food Policy Research Institute, 1999).

22. M. W. Rosegrant, M.S. Paisner, S. Meijer, and J. Witcover, *2020 Global Food Outlook* (Washington, DC: International Food Policy Research Institute, 2001).

23. G. S. Bhalla, P. Hazell, and J. Kerr, *Prospects for India's Cereal Supply and Demand to 2020* (Washington, DC: International Food Policy Research Institute, 1999).

24. M. S. Swaminathan, "Malthus and Mendel: Children for Happiness," *Politics and the Life Sciences* 16 (1997): 219–221; Food and Agriculture Organization, *State of Food Insecurity 2002* (Rome: Food and Agriculture Organization, 2002).

25. Bhalla et al., *Prospects for India's Cereal Supply and Demand to 2020;* see also D. T. Avery, *Filling a Thriving India's Emerging Food Gap* (Indianapolis, IN: The Hudson Institute, 2003); Rosegrant et al., *2020 Global Food Outlook.*

26. FAOSTAT Food Balance Sheets Database 2003 (www.apps.fao.org/page collections?subset=agriculture).

27. Bhalla et al., *Prospects for India's Cereal Supply and Demand to 2020;* P. Kumar, *Food Demand and Supply Projections for India* (New Delhi: Indian Agricultural Research Institute, 1998); P. Gleick, *The World's Water 2000–2001* (Washington, DC: Island Press, 2002); S. L. Postel, *Pillar of Sand: Can the Irrigation Miracle Last?* (New York: Norton, 1999).

28. R. Engelman, R. P. Cincotta, B. Dye, T. Gardner-Outlaw, and J. Wis-

newski, *People in the Balance: Population and Natural Resources at the Turn of the Millennium* (Washington, DC: Population Action International, 2000).

29. S. L. Postel, "Redesigning Irrigated Agriculture," in L. R. Brown et al., *State of the World 2000* (New York: Norton, 2000).

30. S. Bathla, "Water Resource Potential in Northern India: Constraints and Analyses of Price and Non-Price Solutions," *Environment, Development and Sustainability* 1 (1999): 105–121; L. R. Brown and B. Halweil, *Populations Outrunning Water Supplies* (Washington, DC: Worldwatch Institute, 1999).

31. Myers and Kent, "New Consumers: The Influence of Affluence on the Environment"; Tata Energy Research Institute, *Defining an Integrated Energy Strategy for India.*

32. Tata Energy Research Institute, *Defining an Integrated Energy Strategy for India.*

33. R. Ramanathan and J. K. Parikh, "Transport Sector in India: An Analysis in the Context of Sustainable Development," *Transport Policy* 6 (1999): 35–45; R. Bartlett and M. C. Sharma, *India: A Country of Transport Extremes* (Jaipur, India: M. C. Sharma and Associates, 2002); R. K. Bose, *Automobiles and Environmental Sustainability: Issues and Options for Developing Countries* (New Delhi: Tata Energy Research Institute, 1999); J. P. Singh, *Challenges of Urbanization and Environmental Degradation in India* (Patna, India: Department of Sociology, Patna University, 2001).

34. C. Brandon and K. Hommann, "The Costs of Inaction: Valuing the Economy-Wide Cost of Environmental Degradation in India," in L. Fu-Chen, T. Morita, and S. Shishido, eds., *The Sustainable Future of the Global System: Issues, Models and Prospects* (Tokyo: Institute for Advanced Studies, United Nations University, 1999).

35. R. K. Pachauri and P. V. Sridharan, eds., *Looking Back to Think Ahead* (New Delhi: Tata Energy Research Institute, 1998).

36. A. Agarwal and S. Narain, *Trade, Sustainable Consumption and the Environment* (New Delhi: Centre for Science and the Environment, 1996); Brandon and Hommann, "The Costs of Inaction: Valuing the Economy-Wide Cost of Environmental Degradation in India"; E. Brandsma, "Sustainable Consumption Patterns: Global Trends and Events," in San-Whan Lho, Hyun-Jung Im, and R. W. Kim, eds., *Sustainable Consumption Patterns: Trends and Traditions in East Asia* (Seoul: Korea Environment Institute, 1999), 125–138; M. G. Rajan, *Global Environmental Politics: India and the North-South Politics of Global Environmental Issues* (Oxford: Oxford University Press, 1999).

37. J. Parikh and K. Parikh, *Accounting for Environmental Degradation: A Case Study of India* (Tokyo: Institute for Advanced Studies, United Nations University, 2001); A. Takahiro and Y. Nakamura, *Green GDP Estimates in China, Indonesia and Japan* (Tokyo: Institute for Advanced Studies, United Nations University, 2000).

38. A. Agarwal and S. Narain, "When Wealth is Not Health," *Down to Earth* 7(17) (1999): 32–40.

39. World Bank, *Global Economic Prospects and the Developing Countries* (Washington, DC: The World Bank, 2001).

40. T. Palanivel, *Sustainable Development of China, India and Indonesia: Trends and Responses* (Tokyo: Institute of Advanced Studies, United Nations University, 2001).

41. Centre for Science and Environment, *State of India's Environment: The Citizens' Fifth Report* (New Delhi: Centre for Science and Environment, 2001).

42. D. Sperling and R. Bozy, *Limiting Greenhouse Gases in India and China* (Davis, CA: Institute of Transportation Studies, University of California, 2002).

43. R. K. Pachauri, *Beyond KG Gas and Iraq: An Energy Strategy for India* (New Delhi: Tata Energy Research Institute, 2002); R. K. Pachauri and J. Spreng, "Direct and Indirect Energy Requirements of Households in India," *Energy Policy* 30 (2002): 511–523; S. Reddy and P. Balachandra, "A Sustainable Energy Strategy for India Revisited," *Economic and Political Weekly*, December 28, 2002.

44. R. K. Pachauri, *Beyond KG Gas and Iraq: An Energy Strategy for India.*

45. J. Parikh, M. Panda, and N. S. Murthy, "Consumption Pattern by Income Groups and Carbon Dioxide Implications for India, 1990–2010," *International Journal of Global Energy Issues* 9 (1997).

46. Energy Information Administration, *International Energy Outlook 2003* (Washington, DC: U.S. Department of Energy, 2003).

47. K. S. K. Kumar and J. Parikh, "Socio-Economic Impacts of Climate Change on Indian Agriculture," *International Review for Environmental Strategies* 2 (2001): 277–293; T. Palanivel, *Implementation of Agenda 21 in Developing Countries;* Parikh et al., *Consumption Pattern by Income Groups and Carbon Dioxide Implications for India, 1990–2010.*

48. N. Myers, "Environmental Refugees: Our Latest Understanding," *Philosophical Transactions of the Royal Society B* 356 (2001): 16.1–16.5.

49. Energy Information Administration, *International Energy Outlook 2003;* Tata Energy Research Institute, *Partnerships for Sustainable Energy Development in India* (New Delhi: TERI, 1999).

50. N. Myers and J. Kent, *Perverse Subsidies: How Tax Dollars Can Undercut the Environment and the Economy* (Washington, DC: Island Press, 2001); World Bank, *Expanding the Measure of Wealth: Indicators of Environmentally Sustainable Development* (Washington, DC: The World Bank, 1997).

51. International Energy Agency, *World Energy Outlook: Looking at Energy Subsidies; Getting the Prices Right* (Paris: IEA, 1999).

52. Http://pikespeak.uccs.edu/pipermail/assam/2003-March/000129.html.

53. Waldman, A. 2002. "Gates Pledges $100 Million to Fight AIDS." *News India-Times* Online (www.newsindia-times.com/2002/11/22/tow-top21.html).

54. Waldman, A. 2002. "Gates Offers India $100 Million to Fight AIDS" (*New York Times*, November 12 (www.massiveeffort.org/html/nytnov12.html); Waldman, A. 2002. "Gates Pledges $100 Million to Fight AIDS." *News India-Times* Online (www.newsindia-times.com/2002/11/22/tow-top21.html).

Chapter VII

1. Asian Development Bank, *Asian Development Outlook 2000* (Manila: Asian Development Bank, 2000); International Monetary Fund, World Economic Outlook Database, April 2003 (www.imf.org/external/pubs/ft/weo/2003/01/data/index.htm); N. D. Kristof and S. Wudunn, *China Wakes* (London: Nicholas Brealey, 1998); World Bank, *World Development Indicators 2003* (www.worldbank.org/data/wdi2003/) (2003).

2. International Monetary Fund, World Economic Outlook Database, April 2003 (www.imf.org/external/pubs/ft/weo/2003/01/data/index.htm); R. Newfarmer, *East Asia: Recovery and Beyond* (Washington, DC: The World Bank, 2000).

3. K. Hak-Su, *State of the Environment Report in Asia and the Pacific 2000* (Bangkok: Economic and Social Commission for Asia and Pacific, 2001).

4. A. H. Cordesnon, *Saudi Arabia Enters the Twenty-First Century* (Westport, CT: Praeger, 2003); C. S. Smith, "Saudi Idlers Attract Radicals and Worthy Royals," *New York Times*, December 17, 2002, A3.

5. R. Baer, *Sleeping with the Devil* (New York: Crown, 2003); also "The Fall of the House of Saud," *Atlantic Monthly*, May 2003, 53–62; United Nations Development Programme, *Human Development Report 2003* (New York: Oxford University Press, 2003).

6. International Monetary Fund, World Economic Outlook Database,

April 2003 (www.imf.org/external/pubs/ft/weo/2003/01/data/index. htm).

7. Baer, *Sleeping with the Devil.*
8. Baer, *Sleeping with the Devil;* Smith, "Saudi Idlers Attract Radicals and Worthy Royals."
9. Baer, *Sleeping with the Devil.*
10. Ibid.
11. World Bank, *World Development Indicators 2003* (www.worldbank.org/ data/wdi2003/).
12. Statistics South Africa, *Statistics in Brief, 2000* (Pretoria: Statistics South Africa, 2000).
13. United Nations Population Division, *World Population Prospects: The 2000 Revision* (New York: United Nations Population Division, 2001).
14. J. Forsythe, *AIDS in Kenya: Socioeconomic Impact and Policy Implications* (Rome and Geneva: Food and Agriculture Organization and World Health Organization, 1996); N. Myers and J. Kent, "Food and Hunger in Sub-Saharan Africa," *The Environmentalist* 21 (2001): 49–69.
15. International Monetary Fund, World Economic Outlook Database, April 2003 (www.imf.org/external/pubs/ft/weo/2003/01/data/index. htm).
16. T. Larsson, *The Race to the Top* (Washington, DC: Cato Institute, 2001); E. Luis, "Up and Coming: Brazilian Blacks," *Brazzil Magazine,* August 1999 (www.brazzil.com/cvraug99.htm).
17. World Bank, *World Development Indicators 2003* (www.worldbank.org/ data/wdi2003/); K. Maxwell, "The Two Brazils," *The Wilson Quarterly,* Winter 1999/2000, 50–60; A. E. D. Nery, *Going on a Business Trip to Brazil—A Few Important Hints* (http://correionet.br.inter.net/ eccenery/index2.htm) (2002).
18. M. M. Henry, "A Modest Bourgeoisie Buds in Russia," *Christian Science Monitor,* February 2, 2002; M. G. Sodre, C. E. Cervi, and J. Achoa, *Globalization and Changes in Consumer Patterns,* paper for *Human Development Report 1998* (New York: Oxford University Press, 1998).
19. Energy Information Administration International Energy Database (www.eia.doe.gov/emeu/international/contents.html) (2003).
20. FAOSTAT Food Balance Sheets Database 2003 (www.apps.fao.org/ page/collections?subset=agriculture).
21. Global Insight, *World Overview December 2002* (www.globalinsight.com) (2002); see also International Monetary Fund, World Economic Outlook Database, April 2003 (www.imf.org/external/pubs/ft/weo/

2003/01/data/index.htm); J. S. Tulchin and A. D. Selee, eds., *Mexico's Politics and Society in Transition* (Boulder, CO: Lynne Reinner Publishers, 2003).

22. S. L. Postel, *Last Oasis* (New York: Norton, 1997).

23. B. Kastelein, "Urban Desert: Mexico City Facing a Water Supply Crisis," *Amicus Journal*, Summer 2000, 19; E. Malkin, "Uphill Battle," *Amicus Journal*, Summer 2000, 22.

24. S. R. David, "Saving America from the Coming Civil Wars," *Foreign Affairs* 78(5) (1999): 103–114; E. Ezcurra, M. Mazari-Hiriart, I. Pisanty, and A. G. Aguilar, *The Basin of Mexico: Critical Environmental Issues and Sustainability* (Tokyo: United Nations University Press, 1999); M. J. Mazaar, *Mexico 2005* (Washington, DC: Center for Strategic and International Studies, 1999); J. Simon, *Endangered Mexico: An Environment on the Edge* (San Francisco: Sierra Club Books, 2000).

25. International Monetary Fund, World Economic Outlook Database, April 2003 (www.imf.org/external/pubs/ft/weo/2003/01/data/index. htm); B. Milanovic, *Income Inequality, and Poverty During the Transition from Planned to Market Economy* (Washington, DC: The World Bank, 1998); J. D. Sachs and A. M. Warner, *How to Catch Up with the Industrial World—Achieving Rapid Growth in Europe's Transition Economies* (Washington, DC: The World Bank, 2000).

26. International Monetary Fund, World Economic Outlook Database, April 2003 (www.imf.org/external/pubs/ft/weo/2003/01/data/index. htm); W. Lewis, *Russia's Survival of the Weakest* (Amsterdam: McKinsey Global Institute, 1999).

27. L. Aron, *In Search of a Russian Middle Class* (Washington, DC: American Enterprise Institute for Public Policy Research, 2000).

28. Y. Atal, ed., *Poverty in Transition and Transition in Poverty: Recent Developments in Hungary, Bulgaria, Romania, Georgia, Russia, Mongolia* (Paris: UNESCO, 1999); David, "Saving America from the Coming Civil Wars"; A. Elder, *Rubles to Dollars: Making Money on Russia's Exploding Financial Frontier* (New York: New York Institute of Finance, 1999); World Bank, *World Development Indicators 2003* (www.worldbank.org/data/ wdi2003/); Lewis, *Russia's Survival of the Weakest;* V. Mikhalev, "Income Distribution and Social Structure During the Transition," Work in Progress (Tokyo, United Nations University) 16(1) (1999): 14–15.

29. C. Clark, "Russia's Silent Middle Class," CNN Specials (September 1998) (http://edition.cnn.com/SPECIALS/1998/09/crisis.russia/middle.cla ss/); S. Vaknin, *Russia's Middle Class* (New York: United Press International, 2002); W. Lewis, *Russia's Survival of the Weakest.*

30. David, "Saving America from the Coming Civil Wars"; N. Eberstadt, "Russia: Too Sick to Matter?" *Policy Review*, June/July 1999(95) (www.policyreview.org/jun99/eberstadt_print.html); C. Freeland, *Sale of the Century: Russia's Wild Ride from Communism to Capitalism* (New York: Crown Publishers, 2000).

31. Atal, "Poverty in Transition and Transition in Poverty: Recent Developments in Hungary, Bulgaria, Romania, Georgia, Russia, Mongolia"; S. F. Cohen, *Failed Crusade: America and the Tragedy of Post-Communist Russia* (New York: Norton, 2000); D. Iatridis and J. G. Hopps, eds., *Privatization in Central and Eastern Europe* (New York: Praeger, 1998); Elder, *Rubles to Dollars: Making Money on Russia's Exploding Financial Frontier;* Mikhalev, "Income Distribution and Social Structure During the Transition."

32. International Monetary Fund, World Economic Outlook Database, April 2003 (www.imf.org/external/pubs/ft/weo/2003/01/data/index.htm); see also A. Krueger, "Growth and Reform in Russia," address by First Deputy Managing Director, International Monetary Fund, Conference on Post-Communist Economic Growth, Moscow, March 20, 2002; COMCON Research Company, *Lifestyles of the Middle Class* (Moscow: COMCON Research Company, 2000).

33. J. P. Hardt, ed., *Russia's Uncertain Economic Future* (Armonk, NY: M. E. Sharpe, 2003); O. Oliker and T. Charlick-Paley, *Assessing Russia's Decline: Trends and Implications for the United States* (Santa Monica, CA: RAND Corporation, 2002); D. Treisman, "Russia Renewed?" *Foreign Affairs* 81(6) (2002): 58–72; World Bank, *World Development Indicators 2003* (www.worldbank.org/data/wdi2003/).

34. L. Grigoriev and T. M. Aleva, *Is There a Russian Middle Class?* (Moscow: Bureau of Economic Analysis, 2001); World Bank, *World Development Indicators 2003* (www.worldbank.org/data/wdi2003/).

35. Henry, "A Modest Bourgeoise Buds in Russia" ; M. Remizov, "Modernization versus Modernization," *Russian Journal*, April 12, 2002 (http://english.russ.ru/politics/20020413.html); Vaknin, *Russia's Middle Class*.

36. A. V. Yablokov, "A View from Russia," in G. D. Dabelko, ed., *Environmental Change and Security Project Report 7* (Washington, DC: Woodrow Wilson International Center for Scholars, 2001), 93–95; Treisman, "Russia Renewed?"

37. See, for example, C. Kuchins, ed., *Russia after the Fall* (Washington, DC: Carnegie Endowment for International Peace, 2002).

38. Aron, *In Search of a Russian Middle Class; Business Week*, "Snapshots of the Russian Middle Class," *Business Week Online*, October 16, 2000

(www.businessweek.com/2000/00_42/b3703095.htm); Grigoriev and Aleva, *Is There a Russian Middle Class?*.

39. C. Burdeau, "As Economy Grows, So Does Middle Class," *The Russia Journal*, October 26, 2001 (www.therussiajournal.com/index.htm?obj=5171) ; P. Starobin and O. Kravchenko, "Russia's Middle Class," *Business Week*, October 16 2000, 76–81 (www.businessweek.com/2000/00_42/b3703093.htm).

40. G. Diligensky, *The Middle-Class People* (Moscow: The Public Opinion Foundation, 2001); V. Melkova, "Russian Middle Class Hits 25%," *The Russia Journal*, February 3, 2001 (www.therussiajournal.com/index.htm?obj=4158); N. Myers and J. Kent, "The New Consumers and the Influence of Affluence on the Environment," *Proceedings of the National Academy of Sciences* (USA) 100 (2003): 4963–4968.

41. A. Aslund, "Russia's Collapse," *Foreign Affairs* 78(5) (1999): 64–76; Mikhalev, "Income Distribution and Social Structure During the Transition"; Starobin and Kravchenko, "Russia's Middle Class"; see also Russia State Statistics Committee of Russia, *State Statistics 2000* (Moscow: State Statistics Committee of Russia, 2001).

42. United Nations Population Division, *World Population Prospects: The 2002 Revision*.

43. Ibid.; RAND Corporation, *Dire Demographics: Population Trends in the Russian Federation* (Santa Monica, CA: RAND Corporation, 2001).

44. K. Vovk and T. Prugh, "Red Past, Green Future?" *World Watch* 16(4) (2003): 12–23; Yablokov, "A View from Russia."

45. K. S. Losev and M. D. Ananicheva, *Ecological Problems of Russia* (Moscow: Noospher, 2000); K. S. Losev, V. I. Danilov-Danilijan, and M. C. Zalikhanov, *Ecological Security: The Main Principles and the Russian Aspect* (Moscow: International Independent University, 2001); Yablokov, "A View from Russia"; Vovk and Prugh, "Red Past, Green Future?"

46. Energy Information Administration, *Transportation Energy Use* (Washington, DC: U.S. Department of Energy, 2000); McKinsey Global Institute, *Unlocking Economic Growth in Russia* (Moscow: McKinsey and Co., Inc., 1999).

47. McKinsey Global Institute, *Unlocking Economic Growth in Russia;* Energy Information Administration, *Transportation Energy Use.*

48. A. Baumert, R. Bhandari, and N. Kete, *What Might a Developing Country Climate Commitment Look Like?* (Washington, DC: World Resources Institute, 1999); R. Perelet and P. Safonov, "Approaches to Integrated Environmental and Industrial Management in Russia for Sustainable

Development," *Industry and Environment* (United Nations Environment Programme) 18 (1995): 73–77.

49. Elder, *Rubles to Dollars: Making Money on Russia's Exploding Financial Frontier.*

50. FAOSTAT Food Balance Sheets Database 2003 (www.apps.fao.org/page/collections?subset=agriculture).

51. P. Krugman, *The Return of Depression Economics* (New York: Norton, 1999); G. Pauli, *Upsizing: The Road to Zero Emissions, More Jobs, More Income and No Pollution* (Sheffield, UK: Greenleaf Publishing, 1998); Sachs and Warner, *How to Catch Up with the Industrial World—Achieving Rapid Growth in Europe's Transition Economies.*

52. United Nations Development Programme, *Human Development Report 1998* (New York: Oxford University Press, 1998).

53. Central Intelligence Agency, *The World Factbook Database 2003* (www.cia.gov/cia/publications/factbook) (2003); P. French and M. Crabbe, *One Billion Shoppers: Accessing Asia's Consuming Passions and Fast-Moving Markets* (London: Nicholas Brealey, 1998).

54. World Bank, *World Development Indicators Database 2003;* see also A. Argawal and S. Narain, *Economic Globalisation: Its Impact on Consumption, Equity and Sustainability* (New Delhi: Centre for Science and the Environment, 1997); CIA, *World Factbook 2003;* French and Crabbe, *One Billion Shoppers: Accessing Asia's Consuming Passions and Fast-Moving Markets.*

55. World Bank, *World Development Indicators Database 2003.*

56. H. French, *Vanishing Borders: Protecting the Planet in the Age of Globalization* (New York: Norton, 2000); J. R. McNeill, *Something New Under the Sun: An Environmental History of the Twentieth-Century World* (New York: Norton, 2000).

57. M. Sheehan, "Communications Networks Expand," in Worldwatch Institute, *Vital Signs 2003* (New York: Norton, 2003), 60–61.

58. P. Sampat, "Internet Continues Meteoric Rise," in Worldwatch Institute, *Vital Signs 2002* (New York: Norton, 2002), 82–83.

59. Sampat, "Internet Continues Meteoric Rise"; see also CIA, *The World Factbook Database 2003* (www.cia.gov/cia/publications/factbook/geos/xx.html); Nua.com, "How Many Online?" (www.nua.ie/surveys/how_many_online) (2002).

60. United Nations Development Programme, *Human Development Report 2002* (New York: Oxford University Press, 2002).

61. Sampat, "Internet Continues Meteoric Rise."

62. Ibid.

63. A. Gidden, *A Runaway World: How Globalization is Reshaping Our Lives* (London: Profile Books, 1999); N. Hertz, *The Silent Takeover* (London: Heinemann, 2001); N. Klein, *No Logo* (London: HarperCollins, 2000); M. Khor, *Globalization and the South: Some Critical Issues* (Penang, Malaysia: Third World Network, 2000); G. J. Speth, ed., *Worlds Apart: Globalization and the Environment* (Washington, DC: Island Press, 2003).

64. UNAIDS and World Health Organization (WHO), *AIDS Epidemic Update: December 2002* (Geneva: WHO, 2002) (www.who.int/hiv/pub/epidemiology/epi2002/en/print.html).

65. B. Gill, J. Chang, and S. Palmer, "China's HIV Crisis," *Foreign Affairs* 81(2) (2002): 96–110; UNAIDS and WHO, *AIDS Epidemic Update: December 2002.*

66. United Nations Population Division, *World Population Prospects: The 2002 Revision.*

67. UNAIDS and WHO, *AIDS Epidemic Update: December 2002.*

68. Ibid.

69. World Bank, *The Economic Consequences of HIV in Russia* (Washington, DC: The World Bank, 2002).

70. E. Levy and M. Fischetti, *The New Killer Diseases: How the Alarming Evolution of Mutant Germs Threatens Us All* (New York: Crown, 2003); L. Garrett, *The Coming Plague: Newly Emerging Diseases in a World Out of Balance* (New York : Penguin Books, 1994).

71. World Bank, *Global Economic Prospects and the Developing Countries* (Washington, DC: The World Bank, 2001).

Chapter VIII

1. P. Hawken, A. B.. Lovins and L. H. Lovins, *Natural Capitalism* (Boston: Little, Brown, 1999); see also P. R. Ehrlich and A. H. Ehrlich, *One with Nineveh: Politics, Consumption, and the Human Future* (Washington, DC: Island Press, 2004).

2. I. Christie and L. Nash, eds., *The Good Life* (London: DEMOS Collection, 1998); B. Czech, *Shoveling Fuel for a Runaway Train: Errant Economists, Shameful Spenders, and a Plan to Stop Them All* (Berkeley: University of California Press, 2002); N. R. Goodwin, F. Ackerman, and D. Kiron, eds., *The Consumer Society* (Washington, DC: Island Press, 1997); T. Jackson, "Evolutionary Psychology in Ecological Economics: Consilience, Consumption and Contentment," *Ecological Economics* 41(2) (2002): 289–303; M. Jacobs and I. Ropke, eds., "Special Issue on Consumption," *Ecological Economics* 28(3) (1999); J. B. Schor and B. Taylor,

eds., *Sustainable Planet: Solutions for the Twenty-First Century* (Boston: Beacon Press, 2002); I. Wallerstein, *The End of the World as We Know It: Social Science for the Twenty-First Century* (St. Paul: University of Minnesota Press, 1999).

3. Asahi Glass Foundation, *Asahi Glass Foundation News* (Tokyo), February 2003.

4. R. de Young, "Some Psychological Aspects of a Reduced Consumption Lifestyle: The Role of Intrinsic Satisfaction and Competence," *Environment and Behavior* 28 (1996): 358–409.

5. K. Marx, *Wage-Labour and Capital* (London: International Publishing Company, 1975).

6. Jackson, "Evolutionary Psychology in Ecological Economics: Consilience, Consumption and Contentment."

7. M. Silverstein, N. Fiske, and J. Butman, *Trading Up: New American Luxury* (New York: Viking, 2003); J. B. Twitchell, *Living It Up: Our Love Affair with Luxury* (New York: Columbia University Press, 2002).

8. L. Fernandes, "Nationalizing the Global: Media Images, Cultural Politics and the Middle Class in India," *Media, Culture and Society* 22 (2000): 611–628; Twitchell, *Living It Up: Our Love Affair with Luxury;* United Nations Development Programme, *Human Development Report 1998* (New York: Oxford University Press, 1998).

9. D. Korten, *Taming the Giants* (New York: People-Centered Development Forum, 2002).

10. United Nations Environment Programme, *Shopping for a Better World* (Nairobi: UNEP, 2003).

11. J. de Graaf, D. Wann, and T. H. Naylor, *Affluenza: The All-Consuming Epidemic* (San Francisco: Berrett-Koehler, 2001).

12. de Graaf et al., *Affluenza: The All-Consuming Epidemic.*

13. Visit the Web sites of Center for a New American Dream (www.newdream.org) and Redefining Progress (www.rprogress.org).

14. Hawken et al., *Natural Capitalism.*

15. Ibid.

16. K. Geiser, *Materials Matter: Toward a Sustainable Materials Policy* (Cambridge, MA: MIT press, 2001).

17. Hawken et al., *Natural Capitalism;* Factor 10 Institute, Factor 10 Manifesto (www.factor10-institute.org/Publications.htm) (accessed 2003); E. U. von Weizsacker, A. B. Lovins, L. H. Lovins, *Factor Four: Doubling Wealth, Halving Resource Use* (London: Earthscan, 1998).

18. C. O. Holliday, Jr., S. Schmidheiny, and P. Watts, *Walking the Talk: The*

Business Case for Sustainable Development (Sheffield, UK: Greenleaf Publishing, 2002).

19. Hawken et al., *Natural Capitalism*.
20. http://www.famous-quotations.com/asp/acquotes.asp?author= Bill+Gates+(Born+1955)&category=Computers+%2F+Technology.
21. A. B. Lovins, *Small is Profitable* (Snowmass, CO: Rocky Mountain Institute, 2003).
22. K. Kowalenko, "Wind Power Blowing Worldwide," *The Institute* (publication of the Global Energy Network Institute) 26(5) (2002)www.geni. org/energy/library/media_coverage/IEEE/the_institute/fwind. html).
23. G. Gardner, "The Challenge for Johannesburg: Creating a More Secure World," in C. Flavin et al. *State of the World 2002* (New York: Norton, 2002).
24. A. B. Lovins and L. H. Lovins, "Mobilizing Energy Solutions," *The American Prospect* 28 (January 2002); A. B. Lovins, *U.S. Energy Security Linked to Efficiency* (Snowmass, CO: Rocky Mountain Institute, 2003).
25. K. Arrow, D. Jorgenson, P. Krugman, W. Nordhaus, and R. Solow, *The Economists Statement on Climate Change* (San Francisco: Redefining Progress, 1997).

Chapter IX

1. B. Halweil, *Home Grown: The Case for Local Food in a Global Economy* (Washington, DC: Worldwatch Institute, 2002).
2. C. Aslet, "Clocking Up Food Miles," *Financial Times* (London), February 23, 2002.
3. Halweil, *Home Grown: The Case for Local Food in a Global Economy*.
4. Ibid.
5. Center for a New American Dream, "Turn the Tide: Nine Actions for the Planet" (www.newdream.org/tttoffline/actions.html) (2003); J. Getis, *You Can Make a Difference* (Boston: McGraw-Hill, 1999).
6. Center for a New American Dream, "Turn the Tide: Nine Actions for the Planet"; see also Population Coalition, *Our Choices Matter* (Redlands, CA: Population Coalition, 2002); P. R. Ehrlich and A. H. Ehrlich, *One with Nineveh: Politics, Consumption, and the Human Future* (Washington, DC: Island Press, 2004).
7. United Nations Development Programme, *Human Development Report 2002* (New York: Oxford University Press, 2002).
8. United Nations Volunteers, "Volunteerism and the Millennium Development Goals" (www.worldvolunteerweb.org/development/mdg/

volunteerism/UNV_mdg.htm) (2003); United Nations Development Programme, *Human Development Report 2002.*

9. S. B. Breathnach, *The Simple Abundance Companion* (New York: Warner Books, 2000); S. Mills, *Epicurean Simplicity* (Washington, DC: Island Press, 2002); J. M. Segal, *Graceful Simplicity: The Philosophy and Politics of the Alternative American Dream* (Berkeley: University of California Press, 2002).

10. G. M. Bellman, *Your Signature Path: Gaining New Perspectives on Life and Work* (Williston, VT: Berrett-Koehler, 2000); P. Ghazi and J. Jones, *Downshifting: The Guide to Happier, Simpler Living* (London: Coronet, 1997); Getis, *You Can Make a Difference;* R. J. Leider and D. A. Shapiro, *Repacking Your Bags: Lighten Your Load for the Rest of Your Life* (Williston, VT: Berrett-Koehler, 1996); R. K. Leider, *The Power of Purpose: Creating Meaning in Your Life and Work* (Williston, VT: Berrett-Koehler, 2000); J. Schor, *The Overspent American* (New York: Basic Books, 1998).

11. The Harwood Group, *Yearning for Balance: Views of Americans on Consumption, Materialism, and the Environment* (Takoma Park, MD: Merck Family Fund, 1995); see also A. Etzioni, "Voluntary Simplicity: Characterization, Select Psychological Implications, and Societal Consequences," *Journal of Economic Psychology* 19 (1998): 619–643; C. Handy, *The Hungry Spirit: Beyond Capitalism; A Quest for Purpose in the Modern World* (New York: Broadway Books, 1998).

12. C. Hamilton, *Downshifting in Britain: A Sea-Change in the Pursuit of Happiness* (Canberra: The Australia Institute, 2003); C. Hamilton, *Growth Fetish* (Sydney: Allan and Unwin, 2003); Ghazi and Jones, *Downshifting: The Guide to Happier, Simpler Living.*

13. P. H. Ray and S. R. Anderson, *The Cultural Creatives: How 50 Million People are Changing the World* (New York: Three Rivers Press, 2000); Conscious Media, Inc., *About LOHAS* (Broomfield, CO: Natural Business Communications/Conscious Media Inc., 2002). About LOHAS (Lifestyles of Health and Sustainability) on the LOHAS Web site (http://www.lohas journal.com/app/cda/nbp_cda.php?command=Page&pageType=About) (accessed 2003).

14. Gandhi statement March 25, 1969 (www.auroville.org/organisation/supp_statements_india.htm).

15. D. Kahneman, E. Diener, and N. Schwarz, eds., *Well-Being: The Foundations of Hedonic Psychology* (New York: Russell Sage Foundation, 1999).

16. R. Layard, *Happiness: Has Social Science a Clue?* (London: London School of Economics, 2003).

17. R. Rosenblatt et al., *Consuming Desires: Consumption, Culture, and the*

Pursuit of Happiness (Washington, DC: Island Press, 1999); L. J. Y. Thinley, "Gross National Happiness and Human Development—Searching for Common Ground," *Gross National Happiness* (1999): 7–11 (Thimphy, Bhutan: The Centre for Bhutan Studies, 1999).

18. A. J. Oswald, "Happiness and Economic Performance," *Economic Journal* 107 (1997): 1815–1831; T. Princen, M. Maniates, and K. Conca, eds., *Confronting Consumption* (Cambridge, MA: MIT Press, 2002); Rosenblatt et al., *Consuming Desires: Consumption, Culture, and the Pursuit of Happiness.*

19. E. Ayres, "Out of Touch," *World Watch* 15(5) (2002): 3–4; Ehrlich and Ehrlich, *One With Nineveh: Politics, Consumption, and the Human Future.*

20. N. Myers and J. Kent, *New Consumers*, report to the Winslow Foundation, Washington, DC, 2002.

21. R. Layard, *Towards a Happier Society* (London: London School of Economics, 2003); see also D. G. Myers and E. Diener, "Who is Happy?" *Psychological Science* 6 (1995): 10–18.

22. R. M. Worcester, "More than Money," in I. Christie and L. Nash, eds. *The Good Life* (London: DEMOS, 1998), 19–25; see also N. Pidgeon, *Is the Consumer Bubble Set to Burst?* (Norwich, UK: Centre for Environmental Risk, University of East Anglia, 2003).

23. C. Chandy, *The Dissatisfaction Syndrome* (London: Publicis, 2001).

24. G. McCormack, *The Emptiness of Japanese Affluence* (Armonk, NY: M. E. Sharpe, 2001); see also B. S. Frey and A. Stutzer, *Happiness and Economics: How the Economy and Institutions Affect Human Well-Being* (Princeton: Princeton University Press, 2002).

25. C. Graham and S. Pettinato, *Happiness and Hardship: Opportunity and Security in New Market Economies* (Washington, DC: Brookings Institution Press, 2002).

26. Ehrlich and Ehrlich, *One With Nineveh: Politics, Consumption, and the Human Future;* see also D. A. Crocker and T. Linden, eds., *Ethics of Consumption: The Good Life, Justice and Global Stewardship* (Lanham, MD: Rowman and Littlefield, 1997); Leider, *The Power of Purpose: Creating Meaning in Your Life and Work;* Bellman, *Your Signature Path: Gaining New Perspectives on Life and Work;* Handy, *The Hungry Spirit: Beyond Capitalism; A Quest for Purpose in the Modern World.*

27. N. Robins and A. Simms, "Opinion Poll: British Aspirations," *Resurgence*, July/August 2001(201) (www.resurgence.gn.apc.org/issues/robins201.htm); M. Seligman, *Authentic Happiness* (New York: Free Press, 2002).

28. L. M. Michaelis, "Drivers of Consumption Patterns," in R. B. Heap and

J. Kent, eds., *Sustainable Consumption: A European Perspective* (London: The Royal Society, 2001), 75–84.

29. R. de Yong, "Some Psychological Aspects of Reduced Consumption Behavior: The Role of Intrinsic Satisfaction and Motivation," *Environment and Behavior* 28 (1996); N. R. Goodwin, F. Ackerman, and D. Kiron, eds., *The Consumer Society* (London: Earthscan, 1997); Hamilton, *Growth Fetish;* The Harwood Group, "Yearning for Balance: Views of Americans on Consumption, Materialism, and the Environment."

30. Robins and Simms, "Opinion Poll: British Aspirations"; R. E. Lane, *The Loss of Happiness in Market Economies* (New Haven: Yale University Press, 2000); J. B. Twitchell, *Living It Up: Our Love Affair with Luxury* (New York: Columbia University Press, 2002).

31. C. Chandy, *The Dissatisfaction Syndrome;* S. A. Saunders and C. Roy, "The Relationship Between Depression, Satisfaction with Life and Social Interest," *South Pacific Journal of Psychology* 11 (1999): 9–15; T. Jackson and L. Michaelis, *Policies for Sustainable Consumption* (London: Sustainable Development Commission, 2003); R. Levett, I. Christie, M. Jacobs, and R. Therivel, *A Better Choice of Choice: Quality of Life, Consumption and Economic Growth* (London: The Fabian Society, 2003).

32. T. Kasser, *The High Price of Materialism* (Cambridge, MA: MIT Press, 2002); R. E. Lane, *The Loss of Happiness in Market Economies;* Seligman, *Authentic Happiness.*

33. Chandy, *The Dissatisfaction Syndrome;* Layard, *Towards a Happier Society;* Pidgeon, *Is the Consumer Bubble Set to Burst?.*

34. Kasser, *The High Price of Materialism;* J. de Graaf, D. Wann, and T. H. Naylor, *Affluenza: The All-Consuming Epidemic* (San Francisco: Berrett-Koehler, 2001); Robins and Simms, "Opinion Poll: British Aspirations"; Seligman, *Authentic Happiness.*

35. C. Hamilton, *Overconsumption in Britain: A Culture or Middle-Class Complaint?* (Canberra: The Australia Institute, 2003).

36. Layard, *Towards a Happier Society.*

37. P. Drucker, *Post-Capitalist Society* (Cambridge, MA: HarperBusiness, 1992).

38. S. B. Breathnach, *The Simple Abundance Companion;* D. Elgin, *Voluntary Simplicity* (New York: William Morrow, 1993); Etzioni, "Voluntary Simplicity: Characterization, Select Psychological Implications, and Societal Consequences"; B. Schwartz, *The Costs of Living: How Market Freedom Erodes the Best Things in Life* (New York: Norton, 1994).

39. C. Tickell, "Sustainability and Conservation: Prospects for Johannes-

burg," speech to the Society for Conservation Biology, Canterbury, Kent, U.K., July 15, 2002.

40. M. Strong, statement at the hearing of the United States Senate Committee on the Environment and Public Works and the Committee on Foreign Relations, July 24, 2002.

Appendix A

1. J. Lippert and A. Walker, *The Underground Economy: Global Evidence of its Size and Impact* (Vancouver, BC: The Frazer Institute, 1997); F. Schneider and D. Enste, *Hiding in the Shadows: The Growth of the Underground Economy* (Washington, DC: International Monetary Fund, 2002).

2. E. Ayres, "The Shadow Economy," *World Watch* 9(4) (1996): 10–23; B. Bartlett, *Europe's Underground Economies* (Washington, DC: National Center for Policy Analysis, 1998); Schneider and Enste, *Hiding in the Shadows: The Growth of the Underground Economy;* A. Shama, *Notes from Underground: Russia's Economy Booms* (Albuquerque: University of New Mexico, 1997).

3. J. E. Garten, *The Big Ten: The Big Emerging Markets and How They Will Change Our Lives* (New York: Basic Books, 1997); J. Naisbitt, *Megatrends Asia: The Eight Asian Megatrends That Are Changing the World* (London: Nicholas Brealey, 1995).

Index